DEDICATION

To those who continue to make
mention of me in their prayers.

TABLE OF CONTENTS

DON'T CURSE YOUR CRIS

A Faith That Can't Be Tested
Is A Faith That Can't Be Trusted

Michael Pitts

insight *i* publishing group

Tulsa, Oklahoma

N'T CURSE YOUR CRISIS
aith That Can't Be Tested Is A Faith That Can't Be Trusted

n't Curse Your Crisis
Faith That Can't Be Tested Is A Faith That Can't Be Trusted by Michael Pitts
ıblished by Insight Publishing Group
801 S. Yale, Suite 410
ulsa, OK 74137
)18-493-1718

Unless otherwise noted, all Scripture quotations are from the King James Version of the Bible.

ISBN 1-930027-36-2
Library of Congress catalog card number: 2002109796

Printed in the United States of America

For further information contact:

Cornerstone Church
P.O. Box 351690
Toledo, Ohio 43635

www.cornerstonetoledo.com

1 TAKING YOU WHERE YOU WANT TO GO

Don't curse your crisis:
it may take you where you want to go

No season touches the perceptive soul like fall. And I suppose nowhere is fall more vividly comprehended than the Midwest when the last of summer's offerings are withdrawn and the trees yield in submission to the new days ahead by throwing their leaves into the autumn winds.

The moderate days of October in Ohio serve as the friendly reminder, like the soothing voice of a receptionist reminding you of your upcoming root canal on Friday, that the unforgiving days of winter are ahead. The birds know better and fly south while the squirrels go about hoarding their rations.

It was during such a time several years ago that God allowed my soul to be tested to the point of no return. It was for a season, just like winter coming and eventually leaving, but it seemed to me like the longest season on record!

Is there a reason for the season?

I've had many seasons of testing, some harder than others, but I am quick to recognize that all of us are having or will have our own seasons of testing. No one season or test can be used as the template for understanding and dealing with all future seasons and tests. It is simply not possible, anymore than preparing for summer will help you prepare for winter.

Every situation is as unique as the person experiencing it. There are, however, certain similarities, regardless of context, and guiding principles that can cause us to emerge victoriously.

> **Until all that we believe in is tested, we don't truly understand the magnitude or magnificence of what we believe.**

We are giving our attention in this book, not to the proverbial "Why me?" question, but rather to the enlightenment of "What am I now seeing that I did not see before?" This is not the stuff of therapy, but of empowerment! Jesus is the Master Teacher. When we refuse to be victimized by circumstance but rather educated because of its arrival, we trust that each season has purpose and meaning. Therefore, instead of spending our energies trying to escape each season, we seek to extract the hidden messages Jesus is teaching us through the events of our lives. When we are open to His answer, when we are ready to hear it, He will give it!

Times of testing come not to uncover our ignorance but to solidify the things that we have been taught—to bring full assurance that the things we have learned are sound, steadfast, and secure. *The lack of testing is its own witness to ignorance.* The passing of tests are in themselves the qualifying rights to new dimensions of authority. When the teacher is silent and all past information must now be applied, the test is in progress.

Until all that we believe in is tested, *we don't truly understand the magnitude or magnificence of what we believe.* We simply utter phrases without conviction and share clichés void of the experiences that validate them. Oh, how blessed is the man who knows why he believes what he believes!

Blessed? Can a person be blessed in the midst of a test? For some, blessing is as simple as assessing debits and credits—the sum total of all things owed versus all things owned. To others it is so intrinsic that it cannot be identified by possessions or things obtained. Whatever your definition, I believe we can be blessed in the middle of a crisis.

> Could it be that the thing you thought would take you out only serves to bring you in?

Can peace flow like a river when all around is a raging storm? For years I have believed and even preached that blessing is more visible in trouble than in triumph. In my seasons of testing, I've had the chance to experience it and know for sure!

These are the seasons when what we *think* becomes what we *know—for real!*

The right attitude to weather the storm

In the moments of utter confusion and constant controversy, we have the opportunity to believe that we are not the victims of arbitrary circumstance. Instead, we choose to believe that our life has never left the hands of God, the potter, who would fashion us at His own pace and for His own purpose.

Granted, we are not in charge of what happens to us in life, but we are in charge of how we respond to it. In taking the initiative to rise to the occasion, our resolve is resolved. For only those who are pushed to the limits know the limits to which they can be pushed. Only the faith that is challenged is the faith that succeeds.

For all of us, unforeseen circumstances, tragedy, bad news, unexpected turn of events, hardship, and pain enter center stage and produce defining moments. They are the principal players in the drama of our lives.

We despise crisis, resist it, and we do our best to ignore it and avoid it, yet without invitation or apology, it comes. People have always asked, "Why do bad things happen to good people?"

The real question that ought to be asked is, "What happens to good people when bad things happen to them?" I believe good people keep on being good. Their season of hardship often solidifies their goodness, making them even more prepared for greater success than they could have managed had they not been forced to navigate through unfriendly seasons.

Somehow, in the moments following our deepest pain, we rise with a confidence that cuts beyond our injured soul and anchors firmly to our very spirit the belief that God is going to make all things work out together for our good. In the meantime, we must not be afraid to trust our faith in God—and certainly not to fear the God of our faith.

The clarity of crisis

Could it be that the thing you thought would take you out only serves to bring you in? That which you thought would disqualify you miraculously qualifies you. The very thing some thought would kill you and extinguish your flame only made you stronger and caused your passion to burn much hotter.

Is it true that your crisis can become the fuel for your greatest breakthroughs, pushing you, challenging you, upsetting you, but ultimately helping you? Somehow you can come to understand that the crisis only took from you what you did not need and only separated you from those who did not count. It only provoked you in the direction of your destiny. Passivity, indecision, and the luxury of procrastination were snatched from you the moment crisis came knocking at your door.

Though you wouldn't have ordered it, somewhere deep inside, in a place almost untouched by conscious thought, praise is being birthed. Somehow instinctively you know that God is taking you to a place of total trust, without condition and without compromise, where you are just satisfied to know Him and let Him know you.

Maybe that's what He has been after all along anyway.

2   LEARNING TO HANDLE TRUTH

Don't curse your crisis:
it will enable you to handle truth

A lot of what passes for faith these days is actually denial. Reasoning that says, "If I don't see it and don't acknowledge it, then it is not so" is denial, not faith.

What we need, whether we are comfortable with it or not, is a good dose of God's reality. His reality is always truth—and Jesus happens to be the Truth and the ultimate teacher.

Jesus teaches only the truth

Jesus is Rabbi or Teacher, which means that His nature is to teach, and because it's His nature, He will instruct us for the rest of our lives. What's more, because He is the Truth, it follows that the only way He can teach is to tell the truth.

He will never get into denial with us or jump into our psychosis with us. *The problem is that we are not always able to handle the truth He wants to give us.* Most often, we are not able to fully comprehend what He is saying. A sign of maturity is developing the ability to hear what Jesus is trying to tell us rather than trying to get Him to join our own way of looking at things.

How does He take us to that point of maturity? He does it through situations that bring us to the place where we become very receptive to what He is saying to us. In fact, we want to hear it AND we want to do it!

If He presented us with the truth, we would experience a meltdown similar to the time that my wife plugged her curling iron into an electrical outlet while traveling overseas. A few minutes later she picked up the curling iron and it melted in her hand! It simply couldn't handle the increased voltage.

What she needed was the appropriate adapter between the outlet and her curling iron to convert it to the right voltage. That is precisely what Jesus provides us with as He teaches His truths and principles.

The necessity of adapters

Adapters are as necessary in spiritual life as they are in physical life. Here are four common adapters that Jesus uses with us so that we are able to handle His truth:

#1—**The first adapter** is perhaps the most recognized: Jesus speaking in parables. Scripture says, *"And with many such parables spake he the word unto them, as they were able to hear it. But without a parable spake he not unto them: and when they were alone, he expounded all things to his disciples"* (Mark 4:33-34). He knew what the multitudes could handle.

With a parable, you hear it and understand part of it, and then later you get more of it. It is like the adapter with the curling iron; it lets in enough truth and understanding, but not too much so as to cause a "meltdown." When the power source is greater than the instrument, you will always need an adapter. The parables that Jesus used were just that.

#2—**The second adapter** is the representative principle. In the absence of something that God wants us to understand, He gives us something we do understand so that we can draw a comparison and comprehend what it is He is trying to tell us. For example, in the absence of a righteous man, Psalm 1:3 describes him as being *"like a tree planted by the rivers of water, that bringeth forth his fruit in his season; his leaf also shall not wither; and whatsoever he doeth shall prosper."* When laziness abounds, we are commanded, *"Go to the ant, thou sluggard; consider her ways, and be wise"* (Proverbs 6:6).

The Bible is full of these types of comparisons, making His truths a little easier to understand.

#3—**The third adapter** is found in the extremes that God uses to show His truths to us. When the Bible says He made the heavens and knows the stars by name, the picture being painted is that He governs the entire universe with no effort.

Then it goes to the other extreme where He knows when a sparrow falls out of the sky; He knows the number of hairs on your head; and He knows the grains of sand on the seashore. Clearly,

God rules over the universe without a problem, which means He can do anything and everything between heaven and earth. That about sums it up!

#4—The fourth adapter is often reserved for last. It is the fact that what you don't get by revelation, you get by situation. There are truths that Jesus wants us to grasp by revelation, but if we don't, we WILL understand them when we experience them.

Regardless of the adapter, Jesus is the ultimate teacher and He will not let us "graduate" without passing the test. Out of love, He will do what it takes for us to "get it," and that is usually where experience comes into play.

When Jesus' disciples did not "get it"

After the feeding of the five thousand, Jesus sent the multitudes away, then told His disciples to get in a boat and start toward another city across the water. Within no time they were in the middle of a raging storm.

> **What you don't get by revelation, you get by situation.**

Why would Jesus send His disciples into a storm? The answer is simple: they had missed the significance of the feeding of the five thousand. Mark 6:52 says, *"For they considered not the miracle of the loaves: for their heart was hardened."* As teacher, Jesus was not going to let His students move on until they were ready, and since they didn't understand through rev-

16

elation, they were going to have to understand through experience.

It is important to note that a *"hardened"* heart is not an evil heart. A hardened heart is one that is not illuminated. The disciples failed to get (see and understand) what they were supposed to get out of the miracle of the loaves and fishes.

To make matters worse, the disciples didn't even realize that they had

> **If you are rowing against contrary winds, stop right now! Invite Jesus into your "boat" or situation so that you can reach the other side.**

failed to grasp what Jesus was trying to tell them. They didn't get it, and they didn't get that they didn't get it! Jesus gave them two clues about their condition, but that didn't help either:

> **Clue #1**—Jesus told His disciples to go across the lake while He went up the mountain, meaning: *you and I are not going in the same direction.*

> **Clue #2**—Jesus put His disciples in the boat at twilight, meaning: *the further you get away from me, the darker it's going to get because you are headed toward darkness, not illumination.*

What you don't get by revelation, you get by situation, and life becomes a parable. The disciples rowed all night against the winds. Peter, the experienced fisherman, didn't need Jesus' help—or so he thought. Their rowing with all their human strength against the contrary winds was getting them nowhere.

The fact is you can never out-row contrary winds. We have all been in situations where God was saying one thing and we wanted to pursue something else. In my church, for example, God once said that it was time for a season of subtraction and development rather than growth and multiplication. I advertised and brought in several speakers to "kick into another gear" our church attendance, but God didn't change His mind. All my efforts were futile. I was rowing against contrary winds.

Whatever situation it might be, if I try to do anything against it, it never works.

Back in the boat with the disciples, Peter finally got tired. About that time Jesus came walking by on the water. Note that the Bible says Jesus *"would have passed them by"* (Mark 6:48). He would have walked right on past them because He will never follow or join any man's vain attempts against contrary winds. *We follow Jesus, never the reverse.*

When the disciples recognized Him, acknowledged their need of Him, and invited Him into the boat, they were immediately at the other side of the lake (Matthew 14:22-34)!

What the disciples didn't get

The point of the miracle of the loaves and fishes and the storm was the same: what you have in your hands will not get you through unless you invite Jesus into the equation. You can't do it on your own. You must ask Jesus to be involved.

The disciples didn't get it with the loaves and fishes because they were too busy congratulating each other on what a great job they had done. They were probably happy getting into the boat, thinking, "Wow, what a great time we had tonight. Wasn't it amazing! Did you see me flowing in the anointing, breaking bread like that?"

They didn't get it and they didn't get that they didn't get it. But Jesus, being the Teacher, wouldn't let them move on until they got it!

Why crisis will get you to the other side

The awareness of our lack tells us we are about to go somewhere. You don't notice missing keys until you are ready to go somewhere. This produces a seeking that intensifies the closer you are to your time of departure. In our crisis we can become acutely aware of where we are at loss or lack. This awareness and subsequent seeking bring us to the point of truth. The point of becoming aware of things unknown or forgotten. You cannot get to the next level whether it be feeding or sailing without putting it all in Jesus' hands.

3 PROVISION FOR HARDSHIP

Don't curse your crisis:
God made you with a storm in mind

Many Christians have no provision for hardship and find themselves in a theological predicament whenever they encounter a personal crisis. They don't know that God is a God of seasons, that God is a God of time. He isn't as concerned with our comfort as He is with getting out of us the investment He put into us, and bringing authenticity to our faith.

We have segments of people in the Church who believe that if they have enough faith, pray in tongues enough, and live perfectly enough, they will never have any hardship. Then when hardship does come—and it surely will—they are ill-equipped to handle it.

It must be something you did!

When crisis comes, some people believe that something is wrong because they are experiencing hardship. "This shouldn't be happening. I didn't do anything to deserve this," they might say. They reason that their present unpleasant crisis is the result of something they did.

This reasoning, called circumstantial theology, is not valid. Consider the story of Paul recorded in Acts chapters 27 and 28. Paul found himself on board a ship ready to set sail to Italy. He was not the captain or first mate, just a lowly prisoner in shackles. He had been doing the work that God had called him to do, but at that moment in time there certainly was no evidence of external blessing.

> **When the winds are blowing and the rains are beating against your dreams, remember that God built you with the storm in mind.**

Out at sea the ship encountered a storm and began to sink. God gave Paul words of counsel that brought him to the forefront in such a way that all who were on the ship were now listening to him. Had there been no crisis, he never would have been recognized nor his counsel needed.

When the ship sank and everyone made it safely to land (as Paul had prophesied), they found themselves on the Island of Malta. The locals were friendly and helped build a fire for the ocean-soaked men. As Paul was gathering firewood, a snake bit him on the hand.

The locals were masters of circumstantial theology and reasoned: a poisonous snake bit him, therefore he must have done something wrong. As a matter of fact, they concluded that the storm had originally been designed to kill him at sea, and having somehow escaped its wrath, this was God's way of finishing him off.

Their logic didn't hold up because not only did he not die, he showed no signs of the poison affecting him. The locals then changed their minds and declared that Paul was a god! Both of their assumptions were wrong. God was not trying to kill him. He was not a god. At this point Paul spoke up. Despite the fact that he was a prisoner, ship-wrecked, and snake bitten, he preached the gospel, leading many on the island to Christ.

We, who are looking at Paul's story two thousand years later, can see clearly the holes in the circumstantial theology that surrounded him, but let's be honest with our-selves for a minute. If we were arrested, had a car accident, lost our job, received a bad report from our doctor, and dis-covered our house burned to the ground when we returned home, wouldn't we be tempted to hide, pout, complain, blame God, and ask "Why me, Lord?"

In the crisis moments of life, we must remember that we will win if we refuse to quit. His grace is sufficient. It isn't over until it's over—and it's going to be over only when God says that it's over.

> **Only through the surviving of a storm is the value of the foundation of your faith made visible to the most passive observer.**

The fact is storms are a part of life. You can't do any-thing to avoid them and they aren't always the result of something you did. Relax, God sees the bigger picture and He will get you through whatever crisis you face.

Storms are a part of life

The Bible is clear: two houses are built, one on rock and one on sand. For some time, both estates seem compa-rable. Both draw similar compliments from the passersby, and to the casual observer, the buildings are worth about the same. However, seasons have a way of changing.

When the sun disappears, the wind, rain, and flood-waters all take their turn assaulting the two houses. These adverse circumstances are no indication of the strength or viability of the house. Instead, they are just a part of life. The evidence of the house's strength is only visible afterward—when the storm is over.

Of course, the house built on the sand collapses, but the house on the rock is still standing, perhaps even to the surprise of those who never took time to appreciate the foundation! The question is not, "Can the house be built?" but rather, "Can it stand?"

When the winds are blowing and the rains are beating against your dreams, remember that God built you with the storm in mind. He knew rough days would come and He was preparing you for them without your knowledge.

Built with a storm in mind

If God wants to bring to the surface something in us that He has developed for the benefit of other people, they will never see it without the circumstance designed to bring it into visibility. Only after the storm do you know what was built properly.

Provision for hardship is when we come to the place where we realize that God built us with a storm in mind. The man who built the house on the rock knew that the sun wouldn't shine every day. He knew there would be a storm someday!

Build in your heart, mind, and life a provision for hardship. There will be days when everything won't work out. People will lie about you, stab you in the back, your kids will act up, your car will break down, etc. You don't have to worry about it and you can't confess it away. It will come and it will pass. We must have that provision for hardship.

When Noah was building the ark, the question was never, "Could he build it?" The more imperative question was, "Can the thing float?" In times of crisis, we must trust that what is built in us by faith, like Noah's ark, will press through trouble until the storm is over and

> **Often we don't distinguish the eternal from the temporal until the environment that causes the temporary to appear eternal is disrupted.**

what has been built finally lands on a mountain with a new beginning.

Don't curse your crisis; you're more stormproof than you know!

4 DISCOVERING YOUR TRUE IDENTITY

Don't curse your crisis:
for through it you will discover your true identity

In each of us there is a line, however distant on the horizon or buried beneath our composed exterior, a line we most often never think about. It is the line of conditional obedience, the point at which we are no longer willing to follow God.

Most of the time we don't talk about it or really even think about it. We feel committed, unconditionally. Where He leads, we will follow. We trust and obey.

We have become sophisticated enough to know how certain spiritual principles work. We fashion our lives and our theology to fit neatly into the framework we have created that provides us with a certain measure of success and relative comfort. Our knee-jerk reaction to any thought, experience, or relationship that challenges our perfectly programmed lives is to rebuke it, bind it, cast it out, and seek to avoid pain at any cost.

You will find, however, that at the onset of a crisis your comfortableness will be shattered and replaced by frustration. Frustration is the fear your efforts will not "pay off."

We all have a pay-off system with God: If I do this, God will do that. If I do this thing for God, He will do that thing for me. When you are doing all that you know to be right and right things don't seem to be coming your way, it is easy to become frustrated. This frustration brings plainly into view the line of conditional obedience you have drawn.

As we approach this line that we are not aware of, we find ourselves saying, "If God doesn't do this, then..." We have to ask ourselves if we have to have a condition met so that we can obey God. Is there an outcome that must take place before we obey God? Do things have to work out for me to obey God?

God has His own questions, such as, "Will you obey and do what I tell you even if A or B does not happen?"

The once distant line of conditional obedience is now visible.

Raising the level of commitment

A crisis has a way of showing us where our line of conditional obedience is, but that is not all that a crisis reveals. It is during the initial stage of your crisis that the course is set for your outcome.

> **It is during the initial stage of your crisis that the course is set for your outcome.**

During a crisis it is so easy to say, "What's the use?" and throw in the towel or try to negotiate with God. We move from "Why?" to placing certain criteria on our obedience. We hear that nagging voice in our head that says, "If this is what following God is going to do for me, what's the use? Where is the pay-off?"

We expect a return on our investment or at least to know what it will be. God, however, wants to use the crisis to solidify our commitment, to teach us to say "yes" when we don't know what the question is. He wants us to be willing to follow when we don't know where we are going. And even to trust Him when we can't track Him. Scripture says, *"If ye be willing and obedient, ye shall eat the good of the land"* (Isaiah 1:19).

God seizes the days of uncomfortableness and frustration to invade our space. He presses in on us. Unrelenting is His pursuit. Why? Because He wants to deliver us from the bondage of policies, principles, and systems and replace it with a deep personal relationship with Himself.

It may seem as if He is going to take it all—*and He does*—because He wants to be first in our lives. Our human efforts and carefully orchestrated plans fail; the cleverly choreographed music we have been dancing to suddenly comes to a stop.

Now the real issues must be dealt with . . .

- Will you serve Him if people lie about you?
- Will you love Him if you don't get everything you want?
- Can you trust Him when, rather than increase, He hands you the cup of subtraction to drink?

Into the wilderness

Can it be possible, could it be true, that I find myself in the wilderness, not as a result of the devil who is against me, but rather because of God who is for me?

Scripture says:

Therefore, behold, I will allure her, and bring her into the wilderness, and speak comfortably unto her. And I will give her her vineyards from thence, and the valley of Achor for a door of hope: and she shall sing there, as in the days of her youth, and as in the day when she came up out of the land of Egypt.

Hosea 2:14-15

Somewhere, sometime, somehow, as your heart moves forward in spite of present pain, you begin to know He has brought you to this place, not for destruction, but for redemption.

You may not be in crisis because you displeased Him, but rather because there is a greater treasure that must be unlocked within you. In the midst of the wilderness, at the onset of crisis, He is speaking comfortably to you. And somehow you know, and you hope that from this place or experience a vineyard (something of value that will endure) will be born. Don't curse your crisis; it might just be the bus ride taking you where you've always wanted to go.

> You may not be in crisis because you displeased Him, but rather because there is a greater treasure that must be unlocked within you.

God challenges all of the trappings and conditions we have added since our conversion. And before it is over, His promise is that you will sing. So sing in the midst of crisis as you did when

30

you were first saved. Sing as you did before layers of hurt and disappointment silenced your song and before you knew the laws of prosperity, strategies for warfare, or how to be promoted in the kingdom.

Coming out with hope

There is a door in your wilderness, a door of hope. If you will erase the line of conditional obedience, you can walk through it. If you will take the limits off of God, He will take the limits off of you.

Right now, surrender it all to Him. If you are right now in the crucible of crisis, say, "Yes!" Release all of your striving to Him, for restoration is on the way.

Hosea 6:1-3 says:

Come, and let us return unto the LORD: for he hath torn, and he will heal us; he hath smitten, and he will bind us up. After two days will he revive us: in the third day he will raise us up, and we shall live in his sight. Then shall we know, if we follow on to know the LORD: his going forth is prepared as the morning; and he shall come unto us as the rain, as the latter and former rain unto the earth.

That applies to us! The wilderness can be a place of *refining* and *defining*. It is the right of passage you must cross to have your identity securely anchored into who God says you are. The wilderness comes so that you can ultimately do what God said you could do.

John the Baptist is a good example. God took John out of Jerusalem until the day of his public showing. In the wilderness, John learned not to care if people liked him or his message. Some people might have said, "That poor dysfunctional kid. He was raised without his father. Poor thing."

> God puts you in the midst of the rough circumstances to bring out of you something you didn't know you had in you. That something is your identity.

God, on the other hand, took what may have looked like a temporary evil and turned it into a very good and important cause. When John was ready, God took him back to the city of his birth and into his destiny with an established identity.

Identity is set, conditions are not

Do you remember the story of Jesus' baptism in the Jordan River? As Jesus comes out of the water, the Holy Spirit in the form of a dove rests upon Him. Then comes the proclamation of the Father, *"This is my Son!"*

Immediately after this profound moment, Christ is not led into the spotlight to be put on display as God's Son. Instead—just like John—the Spirit leads Him into the wilderness.

There, after an extended period of Jesus fasting, Satan poses to Jesus a question that is in direct antagonism with what God had just stated. Remember that God's last words concerning Jesus were, *"This is my son."* Satan's first words are, "If you are the Son…"

The devil incorrectly points to Christ's condition as the basis of His identity.

I read the story this way: Satan asks, "If you are God's Son, why are you hungry?" This question is offered to us in many forms at many times and goes something like this, "If you are who God said you are, why are you in the condition you're in? If God said you are blessed, why are you broke? If God said you are healed, then why do you feel sick?"

As we are considering our answer, the temptation is to satisfy the hunger of identity with something other than what God has said in His Word about us or about our circumstances.

Back in the wilderness, Jesus gives Satan the answer, *"It is written, Man shall not live by bread alone, but by every word that proceedeth out of the mouth of God"* (Matthew 4:4). The very answer that Jesus gave is the key that unlocks our door of hope when we find ourselves in the wilderness.

Jesus was hungry, but His identity was not based on His hunger, lack, or present condition. He said to Satan, without even addressing His own hunger, "I live according to God's Word and believe what He says about me, regardless of where I am or what I'm doing."

In short, Jesus said, "I trust my Father. I am who He says I am."

Discovering your true identity

You cannot *be* something by *doing* something, but rather *who you are* determines *what you do*. Paul did *not* say, *"I do what I do* by the grace of God," but he did say, *"I am what I am by the grace of God"* (1 Corinthians 15:10). Remember, it is in Him that we live and move and have our *being* (Acts 17:28), *even when we are in the wilderness!*

God calls you and me into the wilderness, not to teach us to *do* something, but rather to *be* someone. The wilderness is a hard place; there are no landmarks, virtually no food or water, and no comfort. It is a place of scarcity, extremes, and isolation. He isolates us from our "support" systems so that we can get our eyes back on Him so that we can realize He knows exactly what He is doing.

> You can find yourself in the wilderness, not because the Devil is against you, but because God is for you.

Who we are must not be built on age, race, income level, or who our parents were or were not. *Being* and *identity* are not based on zip codes, W-2 forms, or other externals. Our identity must be firmly established on who God says we are.

When we know who we are in God, it won't be long until we, like Jesus, walk through the door of hope—out of the wilderness—and return in the power of the Spirit!

When identity is questioned, it is also confirmed. With Jesus' identity firmly established, He entered the temple and once again located Himself in God's Word. He found the place where it was written:

> *The Spirit of the Lord is upon me, because he hath anointed me to preach the gospel to the poor; he hath sent me to heal the brokenhearted, to preach deliverance to the captives, and recovering of sight to the blind, to set at liberty them that are bruised, To preach the acceptable year of the Lord.*
>
> Luke 4:18-19

He then closed the book, sat down, and said, *"Today this scripture is fulfilled!"* Those in the temple began to say, "This is Joseph's son," but it was too late! Jesus had won the battle over identity in the wilderness and He would never be put in their box again.

Don't curse your crisis; because God is going to allow you to discover your identity and to know that no matter what circumstance or environment you find yourself in, you will remain true to who God says *you really are.*

5   FINDING OUT WHO IS ON YOUR SIDE

Don't curse your crisis: it will show you who is really on your side

Many people never know who is truly on their side and who is not. This is vital information, especially when it comes to your inner circle of friends.

There is a desire deep in the heart of every one of us for true relationships that serve not only as a source for encouragement and feedback, but also as safe harbors during the turbulent days of our lives.

Isolation and loneliness plague our culture as our ever-increasing tech-nology seems to reduce us all into the slots of numbers and demographics. We become a collective group known only as

> There isn't anything that can reveal the inward character of someone quite like the pressure of a crisis!

"the market" where we are consumers, customers, and credit card holders. We have business associates, partners, and acquaintances, but do we truly have relationship?

Even among those we call our friends, I think ques-tions of loyalty and concern still exist. We wonder if their love is unconditional. We hope they will care for us even if we are not on top of the world. Will they stand for you? Fight for you? Do they believe in you?

Without the purifying test of crisis, the answer to these probing questions remains a mystery. We know that all those who say they are with us simply are not. Somehow, just under the surface, we instinctively know there are some people who we have allowed into our inner circle who do not have our best interest at heart. Like Adam, we find there is a snake in our garden, or like Jesus, we find we have been feeding our Judas.

Betrayal can be one of the most debilitating emotional tragedies to deal with. The shattering of confidence can linger for years and poison the well you will need for sustaining future relationships. But in a crisis, it isn't the blatant betrayals that hurt so much as it is the quiet passivity of those you so loosely called friends.

We are taught to treat all people the same. When it comes to their intrinsic value or their inherent worth, we should know and observe this. However, all people do not deserve the same placement in your life. There are "outer court" people and there are "behind the veil" people. Otherwise stated, those who are peripheral, casual acquaintances versus intimate friends.

Jesus had the multitudes; He fed them. He never anointed them and sent them. That was for the seventy. Yet out of the seventy He had twelve that He took with Him wherever He went. Of the twelve only three would He take to the mountain of transfiguration. And only one would go all the way to the cross.

Many people live their lives superimposing their desires into relational contexts. Those whom they desire to be their friends they treat as friends. Those who they don't like they treat as enemies. All of us can tell stories, regardless of our feelings, of people that we treated as friends who in fact were proven not to be. A few of us can even tell of those who we treated as enemies, or at least those who appeared to be against us, only to discover they were really for us.

Nothing seems to sift and solidify relationships like trouble. Our feelings, projections, and prejudices no longer cloud our vision. Crisis comes and strips down the scaffolding around the people in our lives—their actions, not our feelings, are plain to see. Many people live their lives never really knowing whom they can count on. Their supposed friendships are weak and shallow—never having been tested they cannot be trusted. Don't curse your crisis; it is going to show you who is really on your side.

Defining your relationships

Crisis has a way of defining relationships while at the same time answering questions that you may have, such as: "Who has God called to be my pastor? Who should I listen to? With whom am I supposed to serve God?" These and other important questions will be answered in a crisis, and that makes crisis a very good thing.

After all, as Scripture points out, *"And we beseech you, brethren, to know them which labour among you, and are over you in the Lord, and admonish you"* (1 Thessalonians 5:12).

Crisis will help you in these three important areas:

#1— Fortifying true relationships—crisis bonds and knits hearts together as nothing else can. If the three Hebrew children who were thrown into the fiery furnace together (Daniel 3) were nominal friends when they went in, they were certainly friends for life when they came out! They had gone through the fire together and their hearts and minds were bonded together.

The same crisis that has the ability to bond you to someone for life has the same ability to rid your life of the person or persons who cannot or will not go through the fire with you. The truth is, those who don't go through the fire with you cannot go to the next level of your destiny. Someone who does not fight with you in the battle should not celebrate with you in your victory.

The people who fight with you in the midst of your battle will be the same people who celebrate with you when you come into your place of blessing! Those are your true friends.

Your crisis will separate the true from the false, those who are truly for you from those who only want the benefits that your sunny days bring to them. Knowing who is on your side is absolutely powerful— and absolutely necessary!

#2—Authority—a crisis will help you identify those who are in authority over you. During crisis, it is not time to run *from* authority, but rather time to run *to* authority. True authority will be a covering and a security in the midst of the storm. True authority speaks authoritatively into your life and your situation, bringing strength into your spirit, soul, and body.

It was in the midst of a crisis that the Prodigal Son recognized his need for a covering of true authority. One day he came to himself and said, *"I will arise and go to my father"* (Luke 15:18). Once he returned to the covering and protection of the father's house,

> **Opinions are distorted over distance. Remove the distance and you might find the person is not as you had imagined.**

everything in his life began to turn around and the things that were broken and out of order were fixed.

Crisis has a way of making you recognize the need for those who have been given true authority over you.

#3—People with good counsel—a crisis will help you define those relationships that God has sent into your life to be instruments of wisdom, good advice, and good counsel. These people have the ability to speak words of wisdom and truth that bring clarity, understanding, hope, and life in the midst of your crisis.

Moving on...and leaving some people behind

It isn't a bad thing to bid farewell to those people who are not called or able to go all the way with you. You are moving on. *They are not bad people!* They were simply there for a season in your life, and that is both natural and fine.

Crisis only reveals what is already there; don't be alarmed. *The people who are called to be with you cannot leave and the people who are not called to be with you cannot stay.* God will never allow to be taken from you (since He's in control and He is leading) something that is essential for your destiny.

I have come to see that if something can be taken from me, then it has God's vote that it is unnecessary. If I go through a crisis and I never hear from a person who I thought would call me, I don't have to be mad at that person. He or she was obviously not essential or necessary to where I am going.

Most people are so afraid of good people walking away from them that they don't fear the mediocre, negative, shortsighted people who are staying with them. We need to let it shake a bit, and in crisis, shaking will take place.

The fact is, the shaking must happen because wrong affiliations and wrong associations impede our walk with God. People who don't want you to grow, change, or move on to a new level are comfortable with you being the way you are—*because they can handle you and control you!* That is not acceptable to you and that is not acceptable to God. A crisis is a great way to open your eyes and break you free from people or situations that are not healthy.

Also, everyone needs to understand that our Christian walk is a journey. When one of us stops walking, we part company. If one of us falls down or stumbles, that's fine, but when someone quits, the other will walk right on past.

Some friends even expire. The dairy products in a grocery store all have expiration dates on them. Certain people are called into your life for a season, and when that season has passed, the friendship is not what it was. It changes, it expires, and that's OK.

Distance distorts

When someone moves on, we often have a hard time disconnecting without demonizing that person. To help ease the pain, we distance ourselves from the offending person—and with distance comes distortion.

Emotional, political, or physical distance distorts our perspective and makes it easy for us to minimize the pain others are experiencing. This explains why in a war situation we individually or collectively seek to distance ourselves from our enemies. We dehumanize our adversary and often demonize them, providing us with the

> The people who are called to be with you cannot leave and the people who are not called to be with you cannot stay.

necessary psychological footings to continue to feel good about ourselves while annihilating other people.

Somehow you expect hostile behavior from your enemies, but when those you have trusted and thought were on your side begin to distance themselves—or worse, turn on you like an enemy—the pain can be excruciating.

It is at this point in crisis that you need to evaluate those who are around you. Instead of pushing away from relationships, pull into what I call "power relationships." Surround yourself with people who:

- are positive
- believe in the highest you
- genuinely want the best for you
- see in you what others cannot (or will not see)
- see the potential of your future and know it will come to pass
- believe in you and the calling of God upon your life, even on the days when you no longer believe in it yourself
- cheer you on through sun, rain, sleet, or snow, yet they also speak the truth in love while at the same time being a cushion of comfort and a shield of protection

These people are a rare treasure indeed, and their worth is far more valuable than gold. And the more gold is purified in fire, the more valuable it becomes. Similarly, true "power relationships" are found in the fire of affliction and the crucible of crisis.

Someone I know went through a crisis and complained afterward, "None of my thirty-three friends stuck with me!" Well, the fact of the matter is that he didn't have thirty-three friends; the crisis showed him that. Now, with that hard-to-swallow revelation, he can take steps to be healed of any hurts and then move on and develop other friendships.

Blessing in disguise

Is there a blessing in the crisis that shakes your friendships to the ground? Absolutely! Most people wander through life with a lukewarm, dispassionate entourage of networkers who have never been forced to take a stand. But crisis has a way of revealing to you, in an undeniable way, those who are really connected to you.

In the Bible, Job's so-called friends could only help him inventory his problems, and in addition, help to assign the blame for the crisis directly on Job himself. And the multitudes that were fed, taught, and helped by Jesus found it to their best interest to keep their distance when their association with Him proved not to be as popular as they initially thought.

On the other hand, there are heroes who have been placed in your life. Unrecognized thus far, they are willing and waiting to rise to the occasion—they just need an occasion.

In either respect, you don't always know who they are and whether they are for you or against you. Even they don't know who they are—until crisis hits. When trouble comes knocking, the politically correct and the self-preservationists take cover while your covenant connections come forward. Those who are called to stand with you will prove their loyalty by taking your crisis personally. They feel as if your crisis is their crisis as well. They take a vested interest in the struggle, and therefore will share in the outcome.

This eye-opening time of crisis can be bittersweet. Some people you thought would always be with you will suddenly excuse themselves from your life while others, whose inward motivations you were never sure of, help you shoulder burdens that by yourself would have been unmanageable.

You simply don't know who is on your side until crisis comes—and you need to know!

6 A PRAISE THAT LEADS

Don't curse your crisis: it may reveal a praise that leads to your victory

In crisis you must find a praise that leads rather than a praise that follows. That is because a praise that leads is the praise that will lead you to your victory. Most of us spend our lives praising God for the things that have happened *after* we have seen or experienced God's goodness. There is nothing wrong with that and it's easy to praise and thank God when we see His mighty outstretched arm parting the Red Seas of our lives.

But what about praising Him BEFORE the Red Sea is parted?

The first record of there being a song of praise in the Bible was when the children of Israel started to sing spontaneously after they crossed through the Red Sea. They shouted, *"I will sing unto the LORD, for he hath triumphed gloriously: the horse and his rider hath he thrown into the sea"* (Exodus 15:1). Until that point, they weren't singing.

To give the praise they gave took no faith. They were praising because of what God had done on their behalf. That type of praise is good and necessary, but that is not the praise that will get you through a tough situation.

Praise requires faith

In crisis you must choose to declare the decree or the promise that God has made over your life. Don't declare the crisis! You must choose to leave the realm of natural sight and sound and choose to agree with the promise of God over your life. Even though you don't know what is going on or why it is happening, even though you don't know how it will work out, you choose to thank Him that He is still God and that He is working all things out for your good.

It takes faith to praise God when the wind is blowing, the waves are raging, and the sky of your life is resounding with the crashes of thunder and bolts of lightening. Though your life may be tossed like a boat in a storm, there must come a sound of praise from deep within.

> Praise of deliverance is good, but it takes no faith. There is another praise that will bring your deliverance— and it requires faith!

All of heaven listens in jubilant rejoicing at the sweet sound of praise given to God in faith.

Crisis will change the way that you praise God

A praise of faith praises before it sees the desired result—*and crisis has a way of pulling this out of you.* In crisis, two things happen:

- You realize that your life depends on how you praise God.
- You get an I-don't-care attitude that says, "Praise God or die!"

If you've never gone through anything difficult, then you don't really know how to praise God in this way. It takes going through something to give you a praise that knows how to endure. This praise knows how to reach beyond what you are facing so that you can get over to the other side and be victorious.

Psalm 103:2 says, *"Bless the Lord, O my soul, and forget not all his benefits."* In other words, you have the opportunity and the potential to forget about God and all that He has done for you. At certain times in your life you become more focused on your problem than on your promise. The Psalmist said, *"I will bless the Lord at all times: his praise shall continually be in my mouth"* (Psalm 34:1). He had the revelation that praise would lead him from crisis to celebration. His praise needed to lead him.

Your praise must get out in front of you for it to lead you to victory.

We see the power of praise illustrated in the story of Jehoshaphat (2 Chronicles 20). The armies of Ammon, Moab, and mount Seir had come up against the children of Israel. Fear had gripped the children of Israel as they pondered their fate in the sight of the enemy. Jehoshaphat called a fast for all Israel and declared, *"O our God... neither know we what to do: but our eyes are upon thee"* (2 Chronicles 20:12).

In the morning as they prepared themselves for battle, Jehoshaphat told the people, *"Believe in the LORD your God, so shall ye be established"* (2 Chronicles 20:20). Then he *"appointed singers unto the LORD, and that should praise the beauty of holiness, as they went out before the army,"* and all the while they were saying, *"Praise the LORD, for his mercy endureth for ever"* (2 Chronicles 20:21).

The children of Israel chose to take their eyes off of their crisis and to place them on the goodness and the promises of Almighty God. As they began to focus upon Him and praise the holiness and mercy of God, they witnessed the power of praise.

The next two verses are incredible:

And when they began to sing and to praise, the LORD set ambushments against the children of Ammon, Moab, and mount Seir, which were come against Judah; and they were smitten. For the children of Ammon and Moab stood up against the inhabitants of mount Seir, utterly to slay and destroy them: and when they had made an end of the inhabitants of Seir, every one helped to destroy another.

2 Chronicles 20:22-23

When it was all said and done, every opposing soldier lay dead on the ground when the children of Israel arrived. And on top of it, there was so much spoil (riches, jewels, food, clothing, etc.) that it took three days to carry it all away!

The lesson for us is that somewhere in crisis, we need to learn to praise God no matter what is going on around us. We begin to sing our outcome before we have any evidence that it will ever come to pass. Praise is prophetic when it is out front and goes first.

Remember what Paul and Silas, locked in the bottom of a prison, were doing *before* the earthquake struck and the doors opened and the chains fell off (Acts 16:25-26)? They were praying and praising God!

Perhaps that is why Isaiah 54:1 says, *"Sing, O barren!"*

Praise that leads is a choice

I can begin to praise my way into a day that I have yet to see and through a battle that I have yet to fight. That is because, as King Jehoshaphat learned, when God arises, His enemies will be scattered. In fact, Psalm 22:3 makes it plain that God inhabits the praises of His people. Inviting Jesus into the situation through praise is exactly what you want!

By focusing on God, you are lifted up and encouraged. By focusing on your problem, the opposite occurs. King David talked about his enemies, but he did not focus on them. He was not a phony or in denial. At times he was surrounded and he acknowledged it, but he kept his focus on God. He wrote, *"Though an host should encamp against me, my heart shall not fear"* (Psalm 27:3).

David didn't count the enemy's weapons. Instead, he focused on God and His goodness and power. When the focus is on God, praise follows.

It requires an active choice of the will to place your praise in front. It certainly isn't something you *feel* like doing. Only through understanding that it is God who fights the battle do we begin to

> **You cannot inherit the Promised Land by taking an inventory of Egypt.**

venture ahead of the soldiers into the battlefield. Armed with praise, we are more ready than we think.

51

Breaking the cycle

Crisis comes so that praise takes its proper place. That proper place for praise is in the beginning, in the middle, and at the end! Until we can praise God in the midst of all of it—when things aren't going as we had hoped—our praise is incomplete.

Practically speaking, if we only praise God when we have a victory, then there will be long seasons when we will not be praising Him. Victory, however sweet it is, lasts only for a moment, while life, "the daily grind," lasts all day long.

> God orchestrates the smallest details of our lives to bring about His desired result.
> Praise Him all day, every day!

We need to be full of praise all the time. Getting our praise out front may be the most difficult, but when we get our praise out front, we will find ourselves entering our Promised Land instead of going around in the wilderness again!

The children of Israel, on the other hand, would wait until good things happened and then praise God. When bad things happened, they would murmur. Here is how it looked:

- They are out of water—they complain.
- Water is provided—they praise Him.
- They are out of food—they complain.
- Food is provided—they praise Him.

God was trying to get them to get their praise out front, but they weren't getting it. When the twelve spies went into the Promised Land, they were supposed to return with a report of how great the land was and then praise their way into this new land that Almighty God had promised them! However, they focused on the giants, on their own we-are-as-grasshoppers condition, and complained. They never made it into their land.

The next generation was told to march around Jericho for six days and be quiet! On the seventh day they were to shout, this time, *before* the walls came down. God was forcing them to put their praise out in front where it belonged.

After all, the essence of the Kingdom is faith. You have to do something ahead of time to get a desired result. Your crisis will reveal this to you, so don't curse it because it may reveal a praise that ends up leading you to your victory!

7 IDENTIFYING WITH THE LEPERS

Don't curse your crisis: it will free you to free others

It seems that before crisis enters people's lives, they only want to surround themselves with people who are successful and without problems. They seem to think that their image and reputation will be tarnished through contact with anyone whose journey has been less than perfect.

They possess a self-righteous attitude that says, "If you had enough faith, you wouldn't be having problems." Yet problems have nothing to do with success and defeat—*and success and defeat have nothing to do with your circumstances*. Success and defeat are attitudes that people carry through life. A person with a defeated disposition will be thwarted by the most trivial of adversities. Conversely, one who is optimistic and possesses an over-coming mentality will rise above the greatest of hardships and obstacles.

Success and defeat are possessed within your spirit. When you have success and victory within your spirit, you look at every obstacle as an opportunity for God to bring His miracle-working power to work in your life. But when you have a defeated spirit, no matter how small the obstacle or how temporary the problem, something in you always wants to pull back and give up.

If you're going to get where God wants you to be, it's not going to be without some obstacles. And many times obstacles come in the form of a crisis.

Before you read any further, receive in your heart now the resolve to press on, keep walking, and overcome. I am praying that as you reach this critical juncture you will not shrink back, turn back, step back, or go back. Your brightest days are ahead. Believe it as a prophetic promise and keep on!

The beauty of crisis

We all want to avoid crisis. We like comfort and convenience, and crisis is anything but comfortable and convenient. When crisis comes, we deny it as if something is wrong with us for having to go through certain situations. We don't want anyone to know that we have bad days. We want them to think that we are perfect, so we put on our mask and say,

> Our message is not that we have our lives perfectly in order, rather, our message is that we have a God who is blessing us while He is yet perfecting us.

"I'm the head and not the tail. I can run through a troop and leap over a wall." All the while we feel like we've been run over by a troop and have run into a wall!

Our message is not that we have our lives perfectly in order, rather, our message is that we have a God who is blessing us while He is yet perfecting us. He's blessing us along our journey. You are not where you are going, you are just on your way there. We've been taught to look toward some great arrival point, but our life is not headed toward one arrival point. We are living a life of consistent arrivals, from one level to the next level.

Through it all, we have somehow attached a false definition to spirituality. We equate spirituality with having arrived at the point where we no longer have any struggles, problems, or adversity. The truth is, the people who don't have any struggles are the people who have already been conquered. The fact that there is a fight means you haven't been conquered. Opposition is merely a sign that you are still in the game.

When you purpose to press toward the mark of the prize of the high calling of God in Christ Jesus, you will discover that there will be a whole host of enemies set up against you. But you have to stir yourself and say, "I am able to arise in the midst of my adversity and win the game." You are playing the game to win—until everything that God has said over your life comes to pass!

Learning to love and relate to others

We also have a tendency to compare ourselves to others. God watches the way we respond to other people's blessings *AND* the way we respond to their failures and weaknesses. Once you see a person's humanness with all of their flaws, God says, "Now that you see the imperfection that I see, will you love as I love?"

Some people don't go to church because they are afraid of the spiritual sheriffs who think it is their job to be Holy Ghost ghostbusters. When you slip, it is their job to pull you over and cite you from the penal code and to explain your violation.

Others are afraid of the self-appointed, vigilante bounty hunters that run through the house of God shooting at everyone.

The Bible says, *"Be not deceived; God is not mocked: for whatsoever a man soweth, that shall he also reap"* (Galatians 6:7). If your brother is overtaken and falls and you are spiritual, you are supposed to restore him. It is our job to seek to restore those in the body of Christ. Be a restorer, not a judge, and recognize that you are moving toward maturity when you recognize your own humanness.

> No crisis,
> no hardship, no change.

Jesus—a friend of sinners

We have been called to identify with people in their crisis. Jesus was known as a friend of sinners. He was not afraid to reach out and touch people while they were in the midst of a crisis. Religious people, on the other hand, act as though a person with a crisis is a leper. And if you are in a crisis, they reason, something must be wrong with you. Under the old covenant, the priests were never able to touch the lepers. If they touched the lepers, the sickness or uncleanness (indicative of sin) contaminated the cleanliness of the priests. The sin was greater than their righteousness.

But when Jesus came, He touched the lepers. Under the new covenant, their uncleanness did not contaminate Him. In fact, Jesus cleansed the lepers by touching them.

Jesus gave us the commission and authority to join Him in His ministry to cleanse the lepers, to remit the power that sin held over them, and to make them feel comfortable in their own skin.

Jesus is our High Priest. He is touched with the feeling of our infirmities because of His own crisis, the cross (Hebrews 4:15). Until you go through a crisis, you don't have the ability to be touched with the feeling of another person's crisis.

Crisis alleviates you from the pressure of other people's expectations. Before you can touch other lives, you learn not to need their approval. You also learn that everyone has to spend some time sitting with the exiles.

Image vs. obedience

Many people have the power to bless or help someone in need, but they are too busy trying to maintain their holy image. In short, they don't want to be contaminated by anyone else's problems and are religiously indignant at the thought of even being seen with someone who has problems.

We tend to run away from those who have problems, but what if Jesus said, "I want you to go join yourself to someone who is struggling?" He might do this—if you are more concerned about your image and reputation than anything else, He might very well do it—for your benefit and for their benefit.

But if we are more concerned with what other people will say about us, we won't reach out to help that person in need. God, however, has a way of breaking through our wall of comfortableness and giving us the opportunity to be the friend of those in need. Jesus said to heal the leper. We are to touch them, help them, and heal them; but we can't do that when our focus is preserving our own righteous appearance.

Removing our arrogance

Crisis produces a broken and contrite heart in us so that we are able to help those who are hurting or struggling—because we don't see ourselves as superior to them. Arrogance is removed. We recognize that we would not be who we are today if it weren't for the grace of God. How can we think of ourselves more highly than we ought?

When you meet a condescending or arrogant person, they have a way of making you know that in their eyes you don't quite measure up. They believe they are something special. But the fact is, they don't know who they are. They have an image that they keep propped up in front of them, but that is not the real them.

Jesus knew who He was and where He was going. Because of that, He was willing to wash His disciples' feet. He ate with the sinners; and He touched the lepers. He also got a lot of flack from those who disagreed with Him. However, He wasn't the slightest bit bothered by those who disagreed with Him. He came to minister to the brokenhearted.

Likewise, when you've been through crisis in your own life and you've been broken, you are willing to help those who are hurting or struggling. You also realize that you don't need anyone's support to befriend the needy. It isn't a concern.

The necessity of change

We need change, because without it, we would never grow. Scripture describes Moab as being *"at ease from his youth,"* having never *"gone into captivity"* (Jeremiah 48:11). Moab never had a crisis, never experienced hardship—and never changed.

To be in captivity with someone is to be inextricably linked to them and to be willing to "chain yourself" to them. You know you could arrive at your destiny more easily and maybe more quickly without them, but because of covenant you refuse to possess it without them, even if you must walk with them until God turns their captivity.

Moab would never say or do that. For him, it was a me-myself-and-I view of life. He will get what he wants regardless of the people or relationships that it costs.

In addition, Moab had never been *"emptied from vessel to vessel,"* which is an analogy of circumstance. In wine making, wine is put in a vessel and the impurities sink to the bottom. Then the wine is poured to the

> **Crisis comes to produce in us a humility and brokenness.**

next vessel. The more vessels (and more time that elapses), the higher the purity and value of the wine, but the fewer the number of vessels, the less valuable and less pure it is. Vessels are the circumstance of life. God pours us from one circumstance to the next. The fewer the circumstances, the less pure our faith as the impurities have not yet been removed.

Because Moab had not been poured from vessel to vessel, *"his taste remained in him, and his scent is not changed."* Like a cup that had a drink left in it too long, you pour in something new and the old taste still dominates. No matter what God might put in Moab, the old taste and smell, or old way of thinking remained.

Since this stagnant unchanged position is not God's best, He says, *"I will send unto him wanderers, that shall cause him to wander, and shall empty his vessels, and break their bottles"* (verse 12). Wanderers are vagabonds, people you are not in covenant with. These individuals will mess up your world, break your bottles, and cause your system to break. If this doesn't happen, no growth will ever come.

From Leper to Leader

Sometimes it's the lepers—the individuals we don't want to talk to or be with—who end up with the revelation or breakthrough. In 2 Kings 7 there were four leprous men sitting outside the gates of Samaria. They were eating donkey heads (indicative of rebellion) and doves dung (leftover moves of the Holy Spirit). The city eventually reached the point where the only thing left was to start eating their own children.

I have seen churches like that—stagnant—and rebellion and leftover moves of the Holy Spirit are all that's left.

These four lepers knew they would not be getting any more handouts. They said to themselves, "Why sit here until we die? If we are going to die, we might as well die as close to food as we can get." They started walking away from their famine and toward a city of abundance.

At that point, the power of God came into action. God took what little they had, in this case the sound of their footsteps, and multiplied it so that the enemy heard chariots and thousands of soldiers. The noise was so great that the people in the city were terrified and ran away, leaving their food still cooking over the fires.

Had the lepers heard the noise, their actions would have required no faith. Instead, they stepped out in faith, only to find a completely deserted enemy camp!

They returned to Samaria with the good news and the entire city was saved as a result. When God says to identify with lepers, do it! It might be a crisis, but it will also be your breakthrough!

Broken before liberated

Anointing flows more perfectly through brokenness. The light of Gideon's army was only visible as their pitchers were broken to reveal it. The woman with the alabaster box could only release the costly perfume by breaking the container that held it. Jesus, like the bread, was broken for us. Don't curse your crisis—it is possible you are finding a level of brokenness that will cause a sweet spirit to be released and a glorious light to be seen, and will prepare you to be given to others.

When we experience our own crisis, our rigid religious attitudes soften. We begin to realize that everyone has hurts and pain. Not every plan will work out the way we want it to. In fact, sometimes being stripped of others' opinion of us by having our reputation damaged can be liberating because it makes us more approachable by those we are supposed to be restoring.

No matter how difficult the crisis, rest assured that God is not "getting you" for past evils. You're not being paid back for yesterday. Some people believe this, but God is a redeemer of time. He is the God of yesterday and He restores the years that the locust have eaten (Joel 2:25). He can reach back into yesterday and take your bad decisions and turn them into a good future.

The truth is, the enemy is trying to stop you because of what tomorrow holds, not because of what yesterday held. The battle is not over your past; it's over your future! *The battle is for your future harvest, and the greater the battle, the greater your future!*

8 YOUR MIRACLE MOMENT

Don't curse your crisis: it is pushing you toward your miracle moment

Many of us never fully understand the value of what crisis can accomplish in our lives. We have come to believe a caricature of the reality of God's kingdom. What we see is not the real picture, but rather a skewed version of reality. Too often we run from difficulties because we have, for whatever reason, come to believe that they are glaring examples of our failure and they have no redemptive value to us or those we love.

The Apostle Paul, however, did not see the kingdom of God from this simplistic viewpoint. In the book of Acts, Paul is the picture of a man pursuing the will of God and yet he was touched by distress and persecution. Though he had seen many miracles, the crowds were easily stirred against him. In one instance Paul was literally dragged out of the city, stoned, and left for dead (Acts 14:19). Immediately after this incident, Paul and his entourage went throughout the region and proclaimed, *"we must through much tribulation enter into the kingdom of God"* (Acts 14:22).

Tribulations in perspective

Paul says that we enter God's kingdom "through many tribulations." In another passage, this very same man wrote the following words: *"For the kingdom of God is not meat and drink; but righteousness, and peace, and joy in the Holy Ghost"* (Romans 14:17).

There is quite a paradox in these two thoughts at first glance, but Paul was revealing a truth that will set us free from the fear of crisis if we can understand it. Here is the truth: *the kingdom of righteousness, peace and joy is entered by enduring tribulation with a right heart.*

That is how God can use for good what the enemy meant for our harm. If we can embrace this revelation, we will do more than just endure difficulty—*we will flourish in it!* We will do more than just look for peace on the other side of crisis—*we will gain His*

> As a result of a miracle moment, your trust and faith in God are strengthened.

righteousness, peace, and joy in the midst of it! So we must look for the redemptive nature of God during our struggles.

When we see from God's perspective the end from the beginning, we see that crisis actually pushes us to the very miracle moment that we have been longing for. What is a miracle moment? Quite simply, it is the place where God intervenes on your behalf and there is no question in your mind that God showed up! It is His incredible power, wisdom, grace, or ability that enables you to overcome.

A crisis or tribulation forces us out of the usual mode in which we operate and causes us to do something out of the ordinary. We find in crisis that the ordinary simply does not work anymore, so we must begin to look for God to do the extraordinary.

Sometimes we do not even know what that extraordinary thing is that God is going to do, but we must learn to trust Him anyway. We may not even know how to formulate an intelligent prayer during this struggle, but that's OK because He can do *"exceeding abundantly above all that we ask or think"* (Ephesians 3:20).

Forcing a miracle moment

Expecting the extraordinary and refusing to remain ordinary is exactly what happened one day in the city of Capernaum. Jesus was teaching in a particular house and those in the city heard about it. The crowd gathered in such

> **If it weren't for a crisis, you would never have your miracle moment.**

great numbers that there was not enough room for everyone to enter, let alone come near the door (Mark 2:1-2).

It was in this setting that four men brought an invalid to the meeting. He could not walk, so they carried him on a bed. Having gone to all this trouble, they found upon arrival that they could not get in to see Jesus. At that point, ordinary methods were out of the question and something extraordinary had to be done. As they were pushed beyond their normal limits, they stepped into their miracle moment.

Here is what they did:

And when they could not come nigh unto him for the press, they uncovered the roof where he was: and when they had broken it up, they let down the bed wherein the sick of the palsy lay. When Jesus saw their faith, he said unto the sick of the palsy, Son, thy sins be forgiven thee.

...And immediately he arose, took up the bed, and went forth before them all; insomuch that they were all amazed, and glorified God, saying, We never saw it on this fashion.

Mark 2:4-5,12

When I read this, it reminds me that there is more to God than what we have seen thus far. No matter how many ways or how many times we've seen God move there will always be more to God than we currently possess or understand.

There is a dimension that God wants us to step into with Him where things begin to happen that will surprise us. In fact, God wants to move through His people in a fashion that is beyond what we would consider normal or ordinary. Yes, we must cooperate with God and work within the principles of God and His Word, but there will come a day where His people proclaim: "We never saw anything like this! We didn't even know that this was possible!"

- It is possible, because of a sovereign move of God, to be so touched by His peace that people will marvel. In fact, it is possible to have a peace in God that others will not understand, especially when the surrounding circumstances are all taken into consideration (Philippians 4:7).
- It is possible, because of the supernatural presence of God, to be so engulfed by the joy of the Lord that we cannot even explain it. At that point God's glory will come on the scene and will raise us to a new spiritual level in spite of the crisis we might find ourselves in (1 Peter 1:7-8).
- It is possible, because of His ability, to comfort and heal and to walk through any valley and any crisis and not be consumed by fear (Psalm 23:4).
- It is possible, because of God's desire to supply, to have every need met to the point where we look around and say: "I could not have even imagined that it would happen this way" (Philippians 4:19)!

How can this be? Sometimes, like the four men carrying their paralyzed friend, crisis pushes us past what is normal and into our miracle moment. We must do things different because the old ways are not compatible with our problem. We must look to God because we are not in charge of this season in our lives. It is beyond us, but it is not beyond Him.

Going beyond what's normal

What did the four men do that was so different?

First, they did not allow circumstances to dictate their responses. Many would have gone home discouraged and disgruntled, saying, "If God wanted me there, He would have made a path in the crowd." But these men refused to be moved by what was normal. They did the abnormal. They refused to be ordinary in the crisis and they anticipated the extraordinary.

Second, these four men took action. They dragged their friend onto the roof and tore a hole in it so large that a man could fit through on a bed (this must have been a little distracting to the message that was being taught down below). Then they lowered their friend down to Jesus.

Third, they took the problem straight to Jesus. Sometimes we must make the effort, as difficult as it is, to lay our crisis at the feet of Jesus. After all, what are we going to do with our crisis? It is greater than we are, so we've got to go to the greater One to get help. The tribulation has already shown us how desperately we need a touch from the master. The mask has been stripped off and the pretense of perfection has fallen away; now the only thing we can do is seek His presence and cry out for a touch from Him.

Fourth, these men refused to be discouraged by the opinions or comments of the people around them. They no longer cared what other people thought about what they were doing. Crisis does that; it frees us from the opinions and expectations of other people. Most have made up their mind about our crisis anyway, so what's the difference?

Notice that these men went to the rooftop, the ceiling, as it were. The ceiling is symbolic of a limitation. It's as far as we go before we bump against something that says: "Stop, no further!"

They went to the ceiling, the limitation, and tore a hole in the limitation. They literally took the limitation off of God. What was some people's peak or pinnacle became their platform. What was the stopping point for the rest of the crowd was where their feet were firmly planted. They were on a level that no one else was willing to ascend to.

Crisis brought those men to a point where they were willing to tear a hole in the limitation that others had put over Jesus. They were now proclaiming: "The ceiling is gone, the obstacles are gone, the sky is the limit for what we will allow you to do to us, for us, in us, and through us. We place our crisis at your feet. We leave the situation in your hands!"

Suffering and difficulty can take us to a new level of trusting God. All of our previous plans, formulas, and programs have failed. The old ways are not cutting it anymore. So now, we must go beyond the limitations of the way we used to do it. We must strip away the boundaries that we have placed on God. We must tear a hole in the obstacles. At that point the pinnacle of where we used to be in God will merely become the foundation of our next level in God. We will know Him better, see Him more clearly, and yield to Him more quickly.

> **You never know Jesus is all you need until He is all you've got!**

And what was the cause of this spiritual breakthrough? How did we reach this miracle moment of peace, joy, comfort, supply, and victory? We, like the four men on the rooftop, laid our crisis at the feet of Jesus and took the limits off!

Crisis pushes you to your miracle moment

There's only one way to have a miracle...and that is to need one!

■ You never know Jesus is all you need until He is all you've got!

- You never know He is a friend that sticks closer than a brother until all your friends quit acting like brothers.
- You never know you don't have to be afraid of the valley of the shadow of death until He takes you down into the valley.
- You never know His strength until you are faced with your own weakness.
- You never know that in Him you are rich until you come to the end of your supply.
- You never understand that you live by His power until you come to the end of your power.

When you are in need and in a crisis situation, you are not relaxing in style. Instead, you are uncomfortable. God forces you out of your comfortableness because He is not committed to your comfortableness—*He's committed to your maturity!* God has put more in you than you'll ever realize. Unless He allows a crisis to push you into your destiny, you'll remain on the stretcher like the paralyzed man your entire life. Crisis has the ability to launch you into the place that God wants you to be.

That is because crisis always preceeds a miracle. There was a famine in the land because Elijah had pronounced that it would not rain again until he said so. It didn't rain for three and a half years and the crisis led him to seek God's provision. The Lord caused the ravens to feed him by a brook. Then he had another crisis when the brook dried up. That crisis in turn led him to the widow woman of Zarephath where the prophetic reward was released and she was able to have her needs met.

It was a crisis that caused the woman with the issue of blood, who had spent all that she had on physicians, to press into Jesus and to receive her miracle.

It was the crisis of being blind that caused the blind man to cry out all the louder for Jesus to have mercy on him.

Your crisis is the prerequisite to your miracle moment.

9 NATURE OF CHANGE

Don't curse your crisis: it is the nature of change

Have you ever seen a skilled landscaper trim a tree? He begins by cutting off or pulling out all the dead branches, then he slowly begins to trim or cut back the outer edges of each branch. As he does, the tree gradually assumes a new shape.

To the untrained eye, some of the cuts seem rather severe, but a seasoned veteran knows which branches are taking up too much of the tree's energy. Those branches must be cut back so the energy can flow to more productive parts of the tree. If you come back to that same tree in a couple of years, you will see a stronger, healthier, shapelier tree in every way.

This process of pruning is both hard on the tree and healthy for the tree's future. If it is cut back too severely, it will die, but if it is left to its own growth cycle, it will not flourish as it could. So, in order for the tree to come to its full potential, it needs some outside assistance. At that point, a gifted landscaper becomes a change agent for the tree's own good, even though the changes he makes cause a season of pain for the plant.

Pruning trees, pruning people

Jesus said:

I am the true vine, and my Father is the husbandman. Every branch in me that beareth not fruit he taketh away: and every branch that beareth fruit, he purgeth it, that it may bring forth more fruit.

John 15:1-2

We are the trees, the planting of the Lord, and He is the "vinedresser," the experienced landscaper. Sometimes we need some outside assistance in order to become more productive for Him. This assistance can come in the form of God sending us into a crisis as He cuts out the unproductive parts of our life and cuts back the productive parts in order to make them more fruitful.

We may be wondering: "Why do I need help in order to grow and change? Can't I do this on my own?" Probably not! Too often we resist the changes that are necessary for our own growth and productivity. We are creatures of habit. We like sameness, routine, and consistency. Anything out of the ordinary can, quite often, mess up our whole day. If it is too much out of the ordinary, then it can send us into a tailspin of grand proportions. As a result, we would seldom choose change as a viable solution.

Change, crisis, and difficulty have this annoying way of encroaching on our comfort zones. They send us reeling as we look for answers to soothe the wounds that are being inflicted. In fact, we will usually resist this encroachment with all of our emotional, spiritual, and physical energy. We may even find ourselves rebuking Satan in the midst of our afflictions.

Later on, however, we learn that it was God Himself, the Master Landscaper, who was clearly at work in our circumstances. He knows that we need to be in a consistent mode of change in order to grow and be more fruitful for Him. The fact is, we are *changed into the same image from glory to glory, even as by the Spirit of the Lord*" (2 Corinthians 3:18). And this requires constant work!

It is His desire that we grow...and that we change

Though we recognize the need for growth, we do not like some of the changes that come with it. So, the Spirit of God steps in to help us change. He knows, better than we do, which parts of our lives are taking up too much of our energy, energy that could be used more productively elsewhere. He knows which relationships are causing us to struggle well past their points of usefulness. He knows which jobs are going to be an emotional and spiritual dead end. He knows which activities, habits, or pastimes are pulling us down and causing us to be less useful to Him than we might be without them. In fact, as God begins to purge us (prune us) of these things in order to liberate us, we tend to call this pruning process our "crisis!" Loss of jobs, loss of certain relationships, loss of extravagant lifestyle, or loss of our coveted reputation are often the very things we are grieving over when the pruning begins, *even though the expulsion of these things from our lives may be just what the Doctor ordered!*

We must remember that the suffering now is far less important than the blessing that will follow. Paul says it best,

"For I reckon that the sufferings of this present time are not worthy to be compared with the glory which shall be revealed in us" (Romans 8:18).

What this means is that we are a work in progress. There are things in our lives that need to be pruned away. The pain of this process is real and feelings of hurt, abandonment, and loneliness can often accompany the experience. Despite these heartfelt emotions, the Lord can deal with them gently and effectively to bring comfort. How? Because He too experienced every emotion that we are feeling now or have felt in the past. Hebrews 4:15 explains, *"For we have not an high priest which cannot be touched with the feeling of our infirmities; but was in all points tempted like as we are, yet without sin."*

Jesus knows about growing pains. He understands the suffering of frail humanity. He tested every emotion, experienced every crisis, and was touched by every infirmity. However, He kept His eyes on the prize. He knows that the fire of affliction is painful as it burns away those things that are not helpful or productive in our lives. But He also knows that what we gain in the fire is more precious to us in the long run than what we lose.

> What we gain in the fire is more precious than what we lose.

The reason for this is *"That the trial of your faith, being much more precious than of gold that perisheth, though it be tried with fire, might be found unto praise and honour and glory at the appearing of Jesus Christ"* (1 Peter 1:7).

We must make a conscious decision in the midst of our trial to allow the Lord to burn away everything that distracts or destroys. We must also allow Him to comfort and encourage us through this process of change and growth because in the end the precious treasure that remains will be glorious.

We will be more focused, more compassionate, and ultimately, more productive. The energy that we wasted in maintaining the old lifestyles, the old relationships, and the old reputation will now be spent productively bringing honor to Him and pointing the way for others who are dealing with their own crisis of change.

Crisis is the nature of change

Crisis is simply the nature of change. It is inevitable, it is coming, and it *forces* change in our lives. Most change does not happen by itself. A crisis is required, one that causes us to do something that we have never done before.

Crisis may be the nature of change, but our nature is that of routine. We are habitual and prefer not to venture too far from the rut that we have paved. This holds true until crisis comes, then we are willing to do anything to get out of the crisis. That is why without crisis, most of us would never change.

Most of us don't like change and may even fear change, but when our desire for the glory of God becomes greater than our fear of change, we willfully choose what is not comfortable. That is because we recognize there is only one way to get to the glory, and that is through change.

When we are vacillating between the two points of desiring the glory and fearing change, crisis comes to help move us toward change. For example, you might be contemplating the fact that you need to pray more, but when crisis comes, you don't need any prodding to change your prayer life—*it will change without any teaching or encouragement!*

It is the very fact that you had to go through something that made you seek God for a word for yourself. Or you couldn't get someone else to pray for you so you had to lay hands on and pray for yourself. Or when you couldn't get anyone to praise God with you, you had to learn to praise by yourself.

It is the fact that you are pressed on every side that pushes you into your destiny. You never really know what's on the inside until the squeeze comes, then whatever is in you is coming out!

But we are creatures of habit who procrastinate. Most marriages in trouble wait until they are almost on the rocks before they ask for help. Families in financial peril seldom seek counsel until there's so much debt that it's almost impossible to dig out from under it.

Then there are those individuals who see a crisis coming and choose to go through it. When they reach the other side, they are stronger and better off than before.

Benefits only found in the fire

There are some things that you have to *acquire IN the fire.* Nobody can explain it, teach it, or give it to you. It must be experienced. You will find that there are some things that you are going to take to the crisis that you are going to leave in the fire. There are also things that you didn't have when you went into the situation that you are going to come out with on the other side of the fire.

Crisis has a way of refining and defining you—anything that doesn't kill you only serves to make you stronger! God has something that He is working out in you because He knows where you are going. God will not allow something to come upon you that will rob you of your destiny. Instead, God has that crisis set up to launch you into your destiny!

Consider Joseph—it was the very fact that Joseph was sold by his brothers that pushed him into his destiny. Little did they know that when they sold him, they actually launched him toward his miracle moment!

Daniel prayed a prayer and an angel told him later that on the first day he prayed his answer was sent. Daniel was in a crisis and kept praying, fasting, and pressing in, even though his miracle took a while to come to pass. Crisis teaches you that you have to pray to stay, fast to last, and give to live. You keep going until you get it!

> **God will not let anything come upon you that you aren't able to bear, so if it's on you, you can bear it.**

Greatness does not happen by itself. Great people are not born—they are made through crisis. And *what you do in crisis* determines what you will do when you come *out of crisis! Your performance will determine your platform!*

10 OUTGROWING YOUR PREVIOUS LEVEL

Don't curse your crisis: it may be the indicator that you've outgrown your previous level

There is no mistaking where the maternity ward in a hospital is located. You can hear the sounds of the crying babies from quite a distance. There is also no mistaking where the birthing rooms are located. The cries of pain coming from there are unmistakable as well.

Giving birth is difficult, to say the least. That is why they call it "labor." It is hard work, as the Bible itself proclaims in several locations, including this description of Rachel:

> *And they journeyed from Bethel; and there was but a little way to come to Ephrath: and Rachel travailed, and she had hard labour. And it came to pass, when she was in hard labour, that the midwife said unto her, Fear not; thou shalt have this son also.*
>
> Genesis 35:16-17

The experience of birth places both the mother and the child in the midst of a crisis. The baby inside of its mother has reached its maximum growth and weight potential. When that child reaches this point, it begins to send its mother into a crisis.

What is interesting, I have found from counseling, is that young couples who have no children often misread the entire birthing process. They begin to declare, "I am not going to have pain during delivery." Note that this is *before* they have been through the process of birth. The veteran mother who has gone through this experience knows that the biblical description of "travail," "labor," "hard labor," and "birth pangs" are more accurate descriptions of the event.

When a woman reaches the stage of transition where the child is just about ready to make its move from the womb to the room, there is a lot of emotional and physical turmoil taking place. Adrenaline is surging, emotions are being expressed, all the senses are on alert, physical pain is at its highest, and everything seems to be at the point of chaos. Signals are being sent from every direction that something new is about to make its entry into the world.

> **Those who accept crisis are also the ones who want to grow to the next level.**

A crisis of growth is occurring and with that crisis comes travail, labor, and chaos. It affects everyone who is around that child, witnessing it move from one level of growth to the next. A crisis of growth sends everyone into a state of transition and flux, especially the mother.

Seeing crisis in a new light

Giving birth may be overused as a metaphor or a little too "earthy" for some, but the parallel is too important and relevant to pass up. Moving from one level of growth to another—just like the baby being born—can cause crisis as well. Those who

> Sometimes our crisis occurs because we have outgrown our previous level and God is trying to bring us into a new, more glorious level in Him.

have settled into a "no crisis in my life" faith decree cannot alter the fact that difficulties can, and do, occur in everyone's life.

But we need to see something else in my earthy example. The event of giving birth to a child has its fill of pain and labor, but it is also an event of great joy. A child is born! Something new and wonderful has entered our lives. A glorious addition has come that we can't imagine living without. Pain, travail, and transition followed by birth, joy, and addition.

Note also that this is not the only crisis the child will experience. The crisis of communication forces the child to talk; the crisis of mobility challenges the child to walk; the crisis of identity as a teenager will cause him or her to look inwardly; and this says nothing of the mid-life crisis as an adult. Each is a trial that if handled correctly will push the individual from one level of growth to the next.

We must begin to see crisis in a new light. We must begin to understand that sometimes our crisis is occurring because we have outgrown our previous level and God is trying to bring us into a new, more glorious level in Him. We have gone as far as we can go in the old and the Lord wants to introduce us to something new.

That new thing, however, cannot fit within the confines of the "womb" of our old experience. So something dramatic has to take place in us before we can be ushered from the old womb to the new room. God wants bigger and better things for us. He wants to expand our vision and increase our influence, but this cannot occur if we remain cemented in the old ways. As a result we are sent into transition.

Accepting crisis for what it is

The pressure and number of contractions only increase during transition, and so it is when we go through crisis. It may even feel like something has gone terribly wrong, is about to break, and is out of control, but that may not be the case at all.

Yes, the pressure of crisis hurts and the emotion of the moment may cause us to get off track and say, "This was sent to harm me!" But we must remember this one truth: *what we think was sent to harm us may simply be the birth pangs of God pushing us into our next dimension in Him!*

Don't curse your crisis! It is simply an indication that you have gone as far as you can go in your current level. Your crisis may be an indication that God is peeling away the old, non-pliable wineskin and replacing it with a new, more pliable wineskin. Then He can pour into you the new wine. Jesus said:

No man putteth a piece of new cloth unto an old garment, for that which is put in to fill it up taketh from the garment, and the rent is made worse. Neither do men put new wine into old bottles: else the bottles break, and the wine runneth out, and the bottles perish: but they put new wine into new bottles, and both are preserved.

Matthew 9:16-17

Why is the principle of the wineskin so important? If we are not willing to be made new, then the new wine simply cannot be poured into our lives. That would be akin to missing the outpouring of the Holy Spirit because we chose to complain about the crisis rather than yield to His transforming touch. James said we should be patient and *"count it all joy"* when we go through trials and temptations (James 1:2-4).

The way to guarantee that you get what God has for you is to embrace the crisis—and trust Him to bring you through.

Always when you least expect it

Have you ever thought of changing careers? Going back to school? Starting your own business? Finding a way to reach hurting people? Becoming a leader in your local church?

As long as we are locked into the routine of maintenance, we have no energy for growth or change. The lack of crisis gives us the luxury of options. And when presented with what it will take to start a business or create a viable ministry versus the relative ease of maintaining the job and ministry we now have, we most often opt to maintain.

Crisis has an unfriendly way of taking away options. If your present joy is lost or current ministry discontinued, it could be the indicator that you have outgrown the previous one. Rather than allow your energies

> **God is not committed to your comfortableness—He is committed to your maturity!**

to be channeled into negative or self-destructive patterns, quickly, before the concrete sets in, do something! Act on those plans and desires you have held for years. When crisis comes, your excuses are gone, your routine has been broken—crisis has freed you.

I knew a man once who lived in a relatively small town. He had been a consistent and conscientious employee for many years. His strong work ethic put him to work on time. He worked hard, and he didn't take gratuitous sick days.

A few years past fifty and contemplating retirement, he was hit with bombshell news: the factory he had worked at was going out of business in a few short weeks. His job would be lost—he would have no retirement. *Crisis had arrived!* But he did have energy, a made-up-mind, and a pickup truck.

He drove his truck to several small businesses in town, owned by people he had known for many years, and explained his predicament. Then he offered to use his pickup to haul away any garbage they may have, and since he undercut the cost of the major competitors, they obliged.

It didn't take long for word to spread that he was reliable, timely, and would even break out a large broom and clean the places where the trash was picked up. Referrals came in and his newfound business began to grow. He also noticed that in many of his rounds there were usable or semi-usable items being routinely tossed out. He began taking those items home to his garage and fixing, cleaning, and painting them.

Soon he needed a second truck to keep up with the demand and he even had to hire some young people as part-time help. Once or twice a year he would sell all the items people had thrown out that he had fixed. Since he had paid nothing for the items and the repairs were minimal, he

> **The lack of crisis gives us the luxury of options.**

was making pure profit. His semiannual yard sales drew increasing crowds and became quite famous in his community.

After a number of years of building up a good client base, still before the age of retirement, he sold his business to a motor company. I was never privy to the final numbers, but I know he helped build an addition on his church and supported missionaries; and he and his wife celebrated a wedding anniversary with stunning multi-carat diamond rings, which they wore proudly while cruising in their new car.

All in all, crisis became his friend. Without it, he would have settled for less, kept to his routine, and retired on a shoestring budget. Crisis took that option away from him and launched him into his next level.

God has a unique way of helping us!

The best is yet to come!

Without crisis, however, we can go on for years, dissatisfied and empty, not really living but just existing. Crisis comes to remind us that we live our lives in tents of flesh, not condominiums of concrete. It announces that there is more land to possess and more dreams to dream. Crisis comes and shows us our weaknesses, our limitations, and the limitations we have superimposed on God.

Somewhere in crisis we also realize the smallness of the space we now occupy. We feel routine is suffocating our faith and our hearts cry out for greater days.

To get there, you have to have a faith that says, "I am in the hand of God and for every door that is shut, another door is opening up. For everyone who walks away from me, somebody else is walking towards me. My crisis didn't do anything but take from me what I did not need and only separated me from people who did not count."

That is faith. God can take something from anyone, but it takes faith to open up your hand and say, "Take whatever you want. Move how you want to move and separate how you want to separate." You say this because you know that on the other side is something new that you have yet to obtain from God.

It is the nature of life that when we outgrow one phase, the way that we are birthed into the next phase is through the transition of contraction and crisis. It forces us into the next level. Though crisis can be painful and can put you in a state that you don't want to be in, recognize that if you are never forced into a crisis, you will never be launched into that next dimension.

Don't curse your crisis. On the other side of your crisis is your greatest miracle; on the other side of your greatest battle is your greatest breakthrough; on the other side of your greatest misery is your greatest ministry; and on the other side of your greatest attack is your greatest assignment!

11 CRISIS DEMANDS ACTION

Don't curse your crisis: it is working in your favor

We all have a natural tendency to avoid pain. Your hand gets too close to the fire and you pull it back. Your stomach begins to rumble and you go looking for something to eat. You are afraid and, as psychologists tell us, you either want to run away or stand and fight.

These reactions, pulling back from the fire, seeking food when we are hungry, and going into the "fight or flight" mode are all very normal. God has placed these responses in us for the purpose of self-preservation. To refuse to act in such a fashion could result in disaster and possibly even death.

Concerning spiritual matters, the same principles apply. We back off, want more, run away, or fight. Similarly, we care about self-preservation. God also cares about us, which is why He put within us certain tendencies to avoid destruction.

Waiting for OUR answer

I once heard a story of a man whose house was being engulfed by a flood. He was a very spiritual man, so he stayed in his house and prayed that God would rescue him from the ravages of the flood.

The first day several men in a four-wheel drive truck pulled up and said to him, "The flood's going to get worse. You need to come with us while the water is only reaching your porch."

He replied, "No, the Lord is going to deliver me."

The second day two more men pulled up in a boat and spoke to him as he stood near the second-story window of his house. They said, "Please come with us. The flood is going to get worse."

He responded, "No, the Lord is going to deliver me."

The third day a rescue helicopter flew over and spotted him sitting on the roof. They shouted down with a bullhorn, "Let us lift you out; your life is in danger. The water is still rising."

He waved them away because the Lord was going to deliver him.

Finally, on the fourth day the flood engulfed his house and the man drowned. When he got to heaven, he said to the Lord, "Lord, I trusted you to deliver me and now here I am in heaven. Why didn't you help?"

The Lord responded, "I sent you a truck, a boat, and a helicopter, but you ignored them all. What type of deliverance were you waiting for anyway?"

Sometimes the answer we want is not the answer that we get. What is our response when that happens? That is what crisis will determine. Take for example the crisis of losing your job. Typically, we respond in one of two different ways, though they are equally as destructive:

First, like the man in the flood, we are so spiritual that we do absolutely nothing in response to the crisis. When the pink slip comes or the business goes down the drain, we sit and wait for God to give us another job. Without saying it, we are waiting for God—though an angel would probably do—to walk up to us and hand-deliver a job offer. We would be better served by preparing our résumé, putting on a shirt and tie, and going out for job interviews. But we do that as a last resort while feeling as if God failed us.

Second, we sink into such a state of despair that we give up completely. We spiritually and emotionally implode. We declare that nothing ever works out for us; everyone hates us; and life is bleak, so why even try. Self-destruction is eminent.

Both of these "solutions" are destructive. God desires that both God and man become actively involved in the process of victory. He will do His part by supplying the necessary comfort, peace, encouragement, and opportunity, but we must do our part by seeking Him, praising Him, and actively preparing ourselves for our breakthrough.

Just what we need: *Crisis*

Crisis may be the very thing we need to push us or motivate us out of our current situation into a healthier more life-affirming atmosphere. It may shake us from the realms of mediocrity into the realms of excellence. Yes, God will aid us in the midst of the difficulty, but we must be actively involved as well. That is because crisis always demands action.

We are also put in the position of making decisions that affect our destiny. Quite often, we have the luxury of procrastination until crisis hits. We're doing a study on our options; we're gathering information; and we may even convince our-selves that we're actually going to do something about the frailties, imperfections and shortcomings very soon. It is not a time for action now, but rather it is a time to ponder.

> **Who we determine to be and what we determine to do are set in motion by our actions.**

All of a sudden crisis hits and the time to make a decision is NOW! No matter how passive we might be, crisis forces us to really deal with the situation. Remember the four leprous men (2 Kings 7) sitting out-side the gates of Samaria? These men finally reached a point where they said, "Why sit we here until we die?" Yes, they needed God's help and He caused the enemy to flee in fear. But it wasn't until the men got up and started walking that the miracle took place. Action was required before the breakthrough came.

The attitude for victory

We must grasp the same attitude as the leprous men when we are in the middle of our own crisis. We need to honestly ask ourselves, "Am I going to hang around with this attitude (these people, this situation, etc.) and die?"

King David understood what it meant to shake off the discouraging attitudes that were always present when facing a crisis. We all fight discouragement and possibly even depression when things don't go our way, but part of the key to victory is taking action to believe otherwise.

In crisis, David knew what to do. The people *"spake of stoning him"* and he was *"greatly distressed"* (wouldn't you be?), but he took action and *"encouraged himself in the LORD his God"* (1 Samuel 30:6). He refused to let depression and discouragement have a part in his final victory. He then sought God and God gave him the answer that turned the situation around in his favor.

He took action even though he didn't know how every detail would work out. He combined the why-sit-here-until-we-die attitude with an attitude that we need to incorporate into our lives as well. It is an

> **Action enables you to shake off feelings of victimization.**

attitude that says, as we are taking action, "Even if what I try doesn't work, at least I'll be closer to where I want to be than where I am right now."

It is a step of faith and it is a step that God wants us to make.

Consider what happened to the leprous men when they took this step of faith. They walked down the road to the enemy's camp and walked right in to find more food, clothes, animals, and other spoils than they knew what to do with. They returned to Samaria with the news and everyone rushed out to plunder the camp. The entire city of Samaria, on the brink of starvation, was miraculously saved!

It took faith; it took action; and it took the right attitude. However, if there had been no crisis, there would have been no victory.

Crisis in perspective

No one likes crisis and you most certainly would never ask for a crisis. Yet crisis can be the best thing that ever happens to you because it forces you to act so that you can get where you are going. It may just be that the very reason the crisis came was to force you to make a decision.

Most decisions to move forward come as a result of a crisis. Most of us would much rather sit in our comfort and convenience, but God is not committed to our comfort and convenience. Instead, He is committed to our maturity, so crisis must come to help us get there.

> **Crisis forces you to make destiny decisions.**

The crisis for the leprous men was the best thing that ever happened to them. As long as the scraps kept coming, they would have sat by the wall, but when the scraps stopped coming, the men made a destiny decision to walk to a place of abundance. It wasn't until their supply was cut off that God opened His supply.

Losing your job, as we mentioned before, is certainly a crisis, but the best job you ever had might just be waiting around the corner. And if you hadn't lost your job, you would still be sitting where you were before. The same applies to any and every crisis situation.

You must remember that God will never take from you anything that you really need and He won't ever separate you from people who are vital for your future. For every door that shuts, another door is opened. For everyone that walks away from you, somebody else is walking toward you. You just have to get up and take action!

> Take action and allow the energy of the storm to drive you to your destiny.

Your crisis may demand action, but the benefits make it entirely worth it!

12 WHAT YOU HAVE OVERLOOKED

Don't curse your crisis: it may reveal what you have overlooked

There is a reservoir of strength in you that you are unaware of—an unwrapped potential that you may have overlooked. You probably don't know how strong you are or what you are truly capable of. You have resident within your heart the power to move mountains and break barriers. Crisis is going to help you locate it!

The Bible recounts a dramatic story in 2 Kings 4 regarding a widow and her sons. The creditor had come to collect on a debt. Being unable to pay, her sons were to be used as bondservants to work until the debt was paid. No doubt darkness and despair closed in on her as her crisis pushed her to seek an answer from the prophet Elisha. Listen to his probing power question.

"What do you have in your house?"

Did you get it? What are you in possession of that you haven't considered? Her answer was simply, "I have nothing except a pot of oil."

There it is! There is a pot of oil in your house as well. Somewhere deep inside of your house the husband of the Church (Jesus) has made provision for you to break the power of the creditor (Satan). Upon His departure He left a pot of oil, a flow of the anointing whose potential you have yet to realize.

Much more than just oil

What did the widow have in her house? What did her husband leave her and his children? What was his legacy? He left them the only thing that he had: the oil of God. Maybe they did not have an economically sound family retirement plan and maybe there were a few more debts than there should have been. But he did not leave them empty-handed. He left them the anointing of the Holy Spirit.

What a marvelous treasure this man, a son of the prophets, handed down to his family. That, I believe, is what Elisha wanted the widow to see. The prophet redirected this hurting woman's focus back to the oil of God's presence and the comfort of God's Spirit.

What did he do next? He told her to go to her neighbors and find every empty vessel she could find. What a stroke of genius! Elisha was not only challenging her to focus on the anointing of God that she had resident within her house, but now he was challenging her to go to her neighbors' houses where there was no anointing, no oil, and no presence—nothing but empty vessels.

> "Thou preparest a table before me in the presence of mine enemies: thou anointest my head with oil; my cup runneth over."
> -Psalm 23:5

Sometimes when we are going through a difficulty we feel very alone and very isolated. We may even feel like there is nobody on earth who understands. Quite often our perspective gets so slanted that we feel like everyone else is doing fine, while we are facing the greatest struggles in the world. But God through the prophet would not allow the widow to stay in this mode. He sent her to people who were even worse off than she was. At least in her struggle she had the "oil of God."

Changing nothing to something

The prophet told her:

> *Go, borrow thee vessels abroad of all thy neighbours, even empty vessels; borrow not a few. And when thou art come in, thou shalt shut the door upon thee and upon thy sons, and shalt pour out into all those vessels, and thou shalt set aside that which is full. So she went from him, and shut the door upon her and upon her sons, who brought the vessels to her; and she poured out. And it came to pass, when the vessels were full, that she said unto her son, Bring me yet a vessel. And he said unto her, There is not a vessel more. And the oil stayed. Then she came and told the man of God. And he said, Go, sell the oil, and pay thy debt, and live thou and thy children of the rest.*

> 2 Kings 4:3-7

The prophet gave the widow a mission: to pour her oil into her neighbors' empty vessels. So, she found as many empty vessels as she could and began to pour, and pour, and pour, and continued pouring until all the empty vessels were full of oil!

Consider the imagery: God's oil, presence, and Spirit came and remained in the house of this hurting family. Then when He had comforted them, He sent them out to minister to, comfort, and pour into the empty vessels of their neighbors. That is how God works.

Notice also that it was the widow's willingness to pour out her oil that eventually brought her breakthrough. She had the choice to never talk to the prophet, let alone do what he recommended. She had the choice to run away and hide her family from continued destruction. She had the choice to lock her doors to the outside world so no one could get to her sons. But she chose to use the oil that was in her house. What she already had became her deliverance, so she poured it into the empty vessels next door.

You have what you need!

What have you overlooked in your crisis? God has not left us without a vessel of oil. There are gifts, abilities, and talents resident within each of us. Yes, there is an anointing for comfort, for peace, and for joy (Isaiah 61:1-3), but there is also an anointing to accomplish great things for God. That is because the oil of the Holy Spirit is not just for the purpose of inward remodeling. The Spirit has been given for outward activation as well (1 Corinthians 12:4).

By using what God has given us, there is an abundant supply available to meet every need (1 Corinthians 12:7). This is exactly what Jesus was explaining to His disciples when He told them the parable of the talents. He explained:

For the kingdom of heaven is as a man travelling into a far country, who called his own servants, and delivered unto them his goods. And unto one he gave five talents, to another two, and to another one; to every man according to his several ability; and straightway took his journey.

Matthew 25:14-15

Some of us may feel that we are not very talented. Others may believe that they have no talent at all, but that is never the case. The kingdom of God, as explained here, is like a man (Jesus) traveling to a far country (heaven), but before He left, He gathered his servants (us) and "delivered his goods to them." Those goods are His gifts and talents as later explained.

We need to refocus, like the widow woman, on the pot of oil that the Lord has left in our house. We need to declare, "I've got the goods. I've got talent! I've got what it takes to survive and flourish!" You may not have what you *want*, but you certainly have what you *need!*

In the midst of your crisis, do not argue with God on whether you have any talents. Sometimes we say, "Oh, I don't really have any talents." We often do this, not because we genuinely believe it, but for the purpose of getting attention. We like to hear people say, "Oh, sure you have talents," and then they begin to list some things we do well. We love that kind of attention, especially when we are throwing a pity party.

Allow me to drive this point home and to plant this seed a little deeper.

Moses has just received the promise and mandate from God that he feels ill-equipped to complete—to deliver the children of Israel. Moses' response to God was, "They will not believe me" (Exodus 4:1).

God then asks Moses, "What is that in your hand?" (verse 2)?

Is it possible there is something you now possess, something you take for granted, something you think is ordinary that God has put within your grasp to be used in an uncommon way?

To catch the full impact of this we must move ahead in time to a place of great crisis. After their dramatic release from Egypt, the children of Israel are at the Red Sea with Pharaoh's army closing in. With nowhere to go, and the people considering stoning him, Moses prays. Once again he has forgotten what is within his grasp. Finally he gets it! Are you getting it?

He says I will stand with the rod of God in my hand. When he uses what God gave him the waters part. I bet Moses didn't realize what he already possessed was capable of producing such a powerful miracle.

Crisis becomes his friend, continually revealing to him he already had everything he needed to set his miracle in motion.

David's rock, Rahab's cord, the little boy's lunch, the jawbone in Samson's hand all serve to show us that we have within our reach what we need. If it's all you've got, it's all you need. God would not allow you to enter a crisis without first providing miracle provision for your victory!

Rise up now, tell your faith to stand up. Declare, "If it's all I've got, it will have to do." Throw your rock, dig your ditch, tie your scarlet cord, pour your oil, blow your trumpet, wave your rod, then stand still and see the salvation of God!

Overlook no more

Your crisis forces you to use what you have been overlooking. You already have what you need; it's already in your house; but you overlooked it. You were relying on someone else, but when crisis comes, you have to look inside and realize there is a pot of oil in your house. God will use it to meet your need.

A pastor friend of mine once told me of a crisis he faced. Unknowingly to the pastor, his Minister of Music had been gathering people together to start a new church. When the pastor walked into church one Sunday, the entire choir, the musicians, and all those under the Minister of Music's authority were gone. They were gone without any warning and without any good-bye. They simply left.

My pastor friend says now that it was one of the best things that ever happened to him and his church, but at the time he didn't know it. That morning as he stood behind the pulpit and told the congregation what had happened, he noticed an individual who he knew could play the guitar. He invited the man to come up and to lead them in a few choruses before the message.

As the man began to play and sing, the anointing of God came into the church and the pastor suddenly realized, "This is what we have been missing, the anointing of God!" The original music team was very talented, but there had been virtually no anointing. It took a crisis to see it.

Just as the widow woman discovered that there was a pot of oil in her house, so too there was a "pot of oil" in my friend's church. *There is also a pot of oil in your house.* Oil represents the anointing of God, and He deposited in you something that you can use to pay off every debt, bless other people, and live off the rest. However, you never tap into it until a crisis comes. Until a crisis comes, you live off of your own strength, education, and employment. But when there is nothing left to help, you find that there is a pot of oil in your house!

> It's what you do *in* a crisis that determines what you do when you come *out.*

Don't curse your crisis because it enables you to find what you have overlooked, and what you have overlooked is more than enough to get you through.

13 Pushing you to your promotion

Don't curse your crisis: it can push you to your promotion

Years ago there was a married couple in charge of a resource ministry in our church. They had always been doing it. They volunteered and they seemed able to handle the details and the inventory. However, over the years they become very possessive of what I had given them charge over. They became increasingly distant from our central vision and even began ordering materials in our resource center that were contradictory to what God was speaking to us. Their critical and contrary spirit eventually was brought to a head. I subsequently removed them and closed down the resource center. Honestly, by this point I did not even care if we ever opened it again.

Not long after this episode, a faithful member presented herself and offered to help with this aspect of the ministry. Her spirit was right, her ability excellent, and under her leadership the next year of that ministry was the greatest ever in our church's history. Each year since then that ministry has continued to grow.

Had crisis not forced me, like most people, I probably would have left "well enough" alone, never dealing with the issues in the hearts of those who were divisive in our ministry. There are some things we put up with and tolerate simply because they are convenient and we are used to them. Crisis helps to break negative cycles and systems and release you toward freedom.

"Behold the dreamer cometh"

In Genesis chapter 37 we find a familiar account in the life of Joseph. Let's look at a portion of it.

Genesis 37:3-11 says:

> *Now Israel loved Joseph more than all his children, because he was the son of his old age: and he made him a coat of many colors.*
>
> *And when his brethren saw that their father loved him more than all his brethren, they hated him, and could not speak peaceably unto him.*
>
> *And Joseph dreamed a dream, and he told it his brethren: and they hated him yet the more.*
>
> *And he said unto them, Hear, I pray you, this dream which I have dreamed:*
>
> *For, behold, we were binding sheaves in the field, and, lo, my sheaf arose, and also stood upright; and, behold, your sheaves stood round about, and made obeisance to my sheaf.*
>
> *And his brethren said to him, Shalt thou indeed reign over us? or shalt thou indeed have dominion over us? And they hated him yet the more for his dreams, and for his words.*
>
> *And he dreamed yet another dream, and told it his brethren, and said, Behold, I have dreamed a dream*

more; and, behold, the sun and the moon and the eleven stars made obeisance to me.

And he told it to his father, and to his brethren: and his father rebuked him, and said unto him, What is this dream that thou hast dreamed? Shall I and thy mother and thy brethren indeed come to bow down ourselves to thee to the earth?

And his brethren envied him; but his father observed the saying.

Authority in a family is ranked from eldest to youngest. According to their tradition, Joseph should be accepting his role as being the servant of all of the other brothers being that he was the youngest at the time. However, something happens in the life of a person when they get a dream.

There is something inside every one of us that tells us that we are destined for more than what we presently see. You need to know that where you're at now is not your stopping place; it's your launching pad!

When you get a dream, you are no longer satisfied with status quo. You're no longer able to be managed and to be manipulated to stay in the circumstance that the dream finds you in. Your dream will always move you towards a greater tomorrow. And the Bible tells us where there is no vision, where there is no open revelation, where there is no dream, people perish.

To Joseph, a seventeen-year-old boy, his dream of promotion was extremely exciting. But not everyone was as excited as he was! His brothers hated him for it.

The Fathering Anointing

The fathering anointing is an anointing of release. It releases you into your destiny because you are secure when you are covered by proper authority. It was his father that released Joseph into the security to dream by giving him a coat of many colors, the symbol of the favor of God that was upon his life. And the favor of the father made him secure.

Garments are symbolic of spirits. So when he covers him with this garment, it's symbolic of the spirit of celebration. Show me people that can't celebrate and I'll show you people without a dream! Show me people with no praise and I'll show you people that aren't going anywhere. When you have a dream and you know God is taking you somewhere, regardless of circumstance, you have a coat of celebration that everybody can see.

Joseph's father gave him a coat of many colors, favored him, and made his son secure enough that when his brothers didn't accept his dream, he could dream on anyway. So Joseph dreamed yet another dream and the next dream was bigger than the first dream! The first dream had to do with some sheaves in the field, but he dreamed yet another dream. This time it was about the sun, the moon, and the stars. It was a dream that was connected to heavenly authority and earthly harvest. God wants to give you some heavenly authority and bring you into an earthly harvest!

His father rebuked him for sharing his grand expectations and his brothers seethed with jealousy. At the first opportunity, his brothers put together a scheme to get rid of this high-minded adolescent. They wanted nothing to do with him or his dreams of leadership. Envy began to cloud their brotherly love as they threw him into a pit, sold him into slavery, and then told their father that a wild beast had eaten him.

The power of a dream

Have you ever wondered why Joseph's brothers really hated him? They hated him for a couple of reasons. Number one, they hated him because they knew his dream was going to come to pass. If you know it's not going to happen, there is nothing to worry about. You only get mad if you know deep inside that it is true.

Secondly, they hated him because he broke his family's cycle and system of dysfunction. Every family has a system that they function by. Each family member has a role to play and as long as each member plays his or her role, the dysfunction game continues. Somebody is the troublemaker; somebody is the peacemaker; somebody is the victim. Whatever the label, each member has a role. But when that family system is broken by the power of a dream, people don't know what to do. They don't know how to play the game unless you play your role. And when you stop playing your role, their little kingdom begins to crumble. So they try to get you back in the game.

They will say, "Don't forget where you came from." But you have been living half of your life trying to forget where you came from so that you can get to where you are going. Or they will say, "Don't ever change; I love you just the way you are." What they are really saying is, "Don't ever change; I can control you the way that you are. I know how to push your buttons. I know how to pull your strings. I know how to manipulate you."

When you get a dream on the inside of you, you step out of your family system and you say, "I'm not playing this game any longer." And when you step out of that circle, everybody else can't play the game because you won't keep it going. And now, they're mad at you because you won't play the game any longer! You broke that system!

When Joseph had a dream, I believe they hated him because he broke their family system. They thought, "You're supposed to be on the bottom; you're the youngest." But Joseph thought, "I'm wearing a coat of many colors; I'm favored; and I have a dream."

His brothers thought if they could take that coat off of him, he wouldn't have a dream any longer. What they didn't know, however, was that once you've worn a coat long enough, you know that even if they take the coat of favor off of you, they can't take it out of you!

Like Joseph we expect those with no dream to get excited about ours. Have you ever had the Lord put something in your heart and you couldn't keep it to yourself? You were so convinced of the purity of other people's motives that you thought they were going to be excited for you, about the dream God gave you. And not knowing what was in their heart, you went running to these people to tell them: "This is what I believe God is about to do." And rather than finding a praise partner, you found somebody who was mad at your dream.

It's hard when you have a dream to understand that everybody doesn't have one. Some people are satisfied. Some people don't mind living in lack and limitation.

Some people don't mind struggling the rest of their life. Some people don't mind scraps from the table. Some people don't mind barely getting through. Some people have built an identity out of making it from one day to the next.

When you don't have a dream, when you don't have a vision, when you have no concept of future, you accept where you are now. And you accept everything in life as the way that it has to be and the way that it's supposed to be.

When you told your dream to other people, they hated you the more, but you couldn't help but dream yet another dream!

One way you know if your dream is from God is whether or not people can kill it. Because if people can kill your dream, God didn't give it to you. You know when you've got a dream that came from God, because when you tell it to people, they try to kill it, and you dream yet another dream!

Joseph dreamed yet another dream and as a result of sharing his dreams, Joseph entered a series of crises that would span some thirteen years leading him to his ultimate destiny!

Coming full circle

When you have a dream you have to risk being misunderstood, sometimes by the very people that you are called to eventually help. When you have a dream you have to be willing to be mistreated and to feel misplaced.

Misplaced, mistreated, misunderstood Joseph has now found himself locked in a prison but with a dream still locked in his heart. While he's in prison, Pharaoh of Egypt has a dream and no one in his kingdom is able to interpret it for him because only somebody with a dream knows how to bring clarity to a dream.

The dreamer's day of deliverance is finally at hand! Joseph is brought up from the prison to interpret Pharaoh's dream. Joseph tells the Pharaoh that God has given him one dream in two parts so that he would know that it is established. Joseph interprets the dream

> **If people can kill your dream, God didn't give it to you!**

and tells Pharaoh that there will be seven years of plenty and seven years of famine.

Famine is the result of improper authority, inordinate government, and a lack of a fathering spirit. Improper authority produces famine. Throughout scripture we see that famines come to bring a shift in authority to place proper authority in position. God uses the famine to promote Joseph into his dream and his proper place of authority. Locked in a place headed for famine is a man with a dream about harvest!

Ephraim and Manasseh

During the seven years of plenty God blessed Joseph with the birth of two sons. The first he named Manasseh meaning forgetful, or "The Lord has caused me to forget the trouble of my father's house" (Genesis 41:51). And the second son he named Ephraim meaning doubly fruitful, or "The Lord has made me fruitful in the land of my affliction" (Genesis 41:52).

Some people are locked into past pain and can't reach their destiny because they won't forget the trouble that their brethren put them through. Before your dream comes to pass, you have to get an anointing to forget. Whatever you continue to remember, you continue to relive. In order to birth your dream, you will have to forget your past!

Not only do you have to get an anointing to forget, but you have to get an anointing to bear fruit in the midst of your trouble. You know when you are healed of your pain when you can look back at your trouble and say, "God gave me some fruit in my trouble that I would never have gotten had I not had to go through what I went through!"

There comes a day when you realize that some of the mess you went through is what made you the strong person you are today. And you are able to say like David, "It was good for me that I was afflicted" (Psalm 119:71). Or like Joseph, "You meant it for evil, but God meant it for my good" (Genesis 50:20). Joseph learned that God put a dream in him of harvest and he couldn't handle harvest if he couldn't handle hardness.

If you are going through some hardness, that means you're getting ready for harvest! At the end, Joseph's dream came true. God shifted the authority and Joseph was put in charge.

Promotion is coming, so don't curse your crisis.

14 ENCOUNTER WITH GOD

Don't curse your crisis: you can't get to your destiny without it

Our ability is an indication of our destiny. God has wonderfully prepared us for our life's work. You've been being prepared all of your life for the greatest work of your life. Preparation is readiness for opportunity. It is not wasted time. Practice helps one perform easily during the critical moments of game time.

Moses—finding his destiny

The way God trains us, leads us, and equips us is marvelous and unique. Somewhere deep inside, Moses knew he was a deliverer. This knowing may not even have risen to the level of conscience thought. Yet it was this purpose to which he was called that drew his attention to injustice. He noticed and pondered the mistreatment of Israel's children.

Why do we notice the things we do? Why do we see what others overlook? Why are we drawn to certain things? Why are we gifted in particular areas? I believe they foretell our callings, they indicate God's intentions.

As the seeds of destiny grew in Moses, and having yet to submit his passion to God's purpose, he sees yet another injustice and acts in the flesh. When he sees one of his brethren being accosted he steps in and murders an Egyptian.

He later encounters the one he protected who showed no gratitude but rather contempt and accusation. In this one scenario the seeds of their collective future can be seen. Moses will seek to deliver and the ones he delivers will complain and resist his authority. If Moses remains untouched by glory he will fail miserably.

God used this crisis to get Moses into the desert off by himself. There for forty years he is being prepared and tempered. He is practicing. He is given the job of watching his father-in-law's sheep—sheep that need to be fed, led, and protected, sheep that go astray and never say thank you. God is forging in him the nature of a man capable of leading His sheep. Can you look back over your life and see situations, jobs, and relationships whose value is only now apparent? Most of our training doesn't make sense in its present context. It only gains meaning retrospectively.

Now that God's time is at hand it is time to transform Moses' natural tendencies into supernatural calling. The agent for this is an encounter with the glory. Moses sees a bush on fire, yet it is not consumed. When he draws near to investigate it the voice of God calls to him and proclaims that Moses is on Holy Ground.

Much could be said and many lessons learned by their brief encounter. However, let it suffice to say Moses was activated that day into His purpose.

As he walks back to Egypt he is empowered! Now his life makes sense. He was raised in the house of Pharaoh; he understands the mentality and culture of the oppressor. He was nursed on the milk of Israel, therefore, he is nourished by identity and knows himself. And now he knows His God and thus knows His calling.

How to get it right the first time

Some people step out of their destiny prematurely because they are impatient or because they think they are ready. Whatever the reason, God will make sure they go back around the same mountain again. Why? Because He is the Great Teacher and He will not let them move on past their level of capability.

Other people try to confess, believe, or give their way out of a crisis season. The fact is *you have to grow your way out of a crisis season.* Seasons come for one reason: fruit! They come so that you can bring forth fruit in your season. Galatians 6:9 says, *"in due season we shall reap, if we faint not."*

Those who try to move on before the season is complete will find themselves in the same season, year after year. Until they develop fruit that is appropriate for that season, they simply can't move on. That is why my attitude is, "God, whatever I need to learn in this season, I want to learn it. I choose to be open and obedient so I can get it the first time."

Have you met people whose lives are suspended in a certain season? If they were to look carefully at their lives, they would see that they've been around the same mountain before. When they begin to realize they aren't learning what they need to be learning, that is when things often begin to change for the better. Some people, however, recognize their situation and still refuse to grow up.

What is the secret to not going around the mountain again? *You have to settle who God is*—He runs the universe; He is in charge; He is in control; He knows everything, and

He is working everything out for His own purpose. When you get that settled, even if you don't like the circumstance you find yourself in, a new level of trust and faith begins to grow in you.

Some people mistakenly see their season as an "arrival" point or destination, but no season is permanent. Instead, life is a process, like a motion picture, not a single snapshot. None of us have "arrived" or will ever "arrive." It's all a journey, which means we cannot set up camp during the good times or during the bad times. We must keep moving forward, and God promises to always take you to the other side.

> **No season is permanent.**

Our testimony as a Christian then is not that we've never stumbled or fallen down, but that we've never stopped walking. The Bible doesn't condemn people who fall, make mistakes, or fail. Psalm 37:23-24 makes that plain: *"The steps of a good man are ordered by the LORD: and he delighteth in his way. Though he fall, he shall not be utterly cast down: for the LORD upholdeth him with his hand."*

The Bible only condemns those who stop.

His help is what gets you through

God upholds each of us with His hand. In fact, we can find comfort in the fact that He is better at holding us up than we are at picking ourselves up. It is His strength and grace that keeps us going, and the sooner we recognize that the better.

Psalm 34:18-19 says, *"The LORD is nigh unto them that are of a broken heart; and saveth such as be of a contrite spirit. Many are the afflictions of the righteous: but the LORD delivereth him out of them all."*

God is faithful to deliver all of those who put their full trust in Him. He is a very present help in trouble! Knowing He is leading gives us security. The truth is that He is better at leading than we are at following. Sometimes to get us to encounter Him in

> **The only way out of a crisis season is to grow your way out.**

His glory He must separate us from our present support systems and draw our focus firmly upon Him. The resulting clarity brings into view purpose, destiny, and the role we will play in God's great plan.

15 PERSONAL REVIVAL

Don't curse your crisis:
it is the fuel to your personal revival

Crisis can become motivation for you. Have you ever considered how many fitness experts were at one time severely out of shape? Did you know Mothers Against Drunk Driving (MADD) was started by a mother who lost her child in a needless accident? After the abduction and murder of his son, John Walsh turned his crisis into fuel and relentlessly pursued criminals through his famous show "America's Most Wanted."

Great thinkers and geniuses were sometimes mislabeled as slow learners. Most inventors failed before they succeeded. Shakespeare once wrote, "Show me a hero and I'll show you a tragedy."

The point is that greatness can be born through hardship. The people we admire, the ones who move mountains, and break barriers, all have a story. And without exception, I have found that though they may not, on the onset of their journey, have seen all the future held, here on the other side they see how integral a part of their success earlier crisis played. By the time you get to where you are going you will be able to lift your voice in testimony with saints of old and with them say, "I wouldn't take anything for my journey now."

When you refuse to curse your crisis, the thing that looks like it was sent to stop you instead ends up pushing you into a personal revival and bringing great change.

From personal revival to bust

Personal revival is not more, and certainly not less, than simply hearing the voice of God in our lives. *There is no such thing as being revived, renewed, or restored if we do not hear Him as He speaks to us.* That, I believe, is why one of the most often repeated thoughts in the entire Bible is *"He that hath an ear, let him hear what the Spirit saith unto the churches"* (Revelation 2:7). We simply cannot experience a personal or corporate revival if we shut out the voice of God.

When Elijah did hear the Word of the Lord, he experienced confidence, and as a result the entire nation was turned back to God. Judgment fell on the false prophets and the name of the Lord was magnified. Why? Because Elijah had heard the voice of God and experienced a personal revival and that personal revival spread to the people.

> **We simply cannot experience a personal or corporate revival if we shut out the voice of God.**

The next day Queen Jezebel threatened to kill Elijah. Instead of the expected boldness, Elijah became very afraid and ran for his life. Not only that, but he experienced such massive depression that he wanted to die. He ran into the wilderness with his servant, then left his servant and traveled another day's journey, by himself, and sat in despair under a juniper tree (1 Kings 19:4). His depression was leading him to isolation.

Just days before he was bold, confident, and standing on top of the world. Now he was fearful, isolated, and depressed. He went from the mountain to the valley in a mere twenty-four hours. The difference? One day Elijah was hearing the voice of God, the next day he was not. The pain, loneliness, and fear were crying so loud in his spirit that the voice of God could not be heard.

Restoring the revival

How did God respond to Elijah? Did God reject him? No, God handled him gently with compassion until Elijah could, once again, hear His voice. That is exactly how the Lord will handle us as well. Elijah was a great prophet, but he is no different than we are (James 5:17).

God did not minister to him any differently than He would minister to us in the midst of our crisis. In fact, that may be exactly what crisis will accomplish in our lives. It will peel away all the peripheral issues so that we may, once again, hear His voice and be revived.

Here was Elijah, sitting under a juniper tree, expressing his desire to die. The Lord sent an angel to minister to him and strengthen him. 1 Kings 19:5-6 says:

And as he lay and slept under a juniper tree, behold, then an angel touched him, and said unto him, Arise and eat. And he looked, and, behold, there was a cake baken on the coals, and a cruse of water at his head. And he did eat and drink, and laid him down again.

Elijah was not even strong enough to respond. He simply ate and went back to bed. It may not seem like much, but sometimes that is all we can do at that point in time. This is an important point. In the midst of crisis, keep eating properly and keep resting. We may not be hearing the voice of God right now, but if we continue to take care of ourselves, we will eventually survive long enough to do so. If we allow the crisis to throw us into such a state of despair that we destroy our bodies, we will only compound the problem and possibly prolong the days that we are in the midst of affliction.

> **Crisis can't do anything but push you into the place that God wants you to be.**

The next day the angel prepared Elijah another meal. This time he was strong enough to continue. In fact, he went *"in the strength of that meat forty days and forty nights unto Horeb the mount of God"* (1 Kings 19:8).

The angel, in the midst of Elijah's crisis, was moving him to the mountain of God's presence. Crisis begins to move us closer to God. God is drawing us nearer, even when we are spiritually, emotionally and physically drained. After forty days of traveling through the wilderness to the mountain of God's presence, the Lord was about to remodel Elijah's perspective. The first thing the Lord asked him was, *"What doest thou here, Elijah?"* (1 Kings 19:9).

You can hear the emotional frustration as Elijah took this opportunity to unload:

I have been very jealous for the LORD God of hosts: for the children of Israel have forsaken thy covenant, thrown down thine altars, and slain thy prophets with the sword; and I, even I only, am left; and they seek my life, to take it away.

1 Kings 19:10

God, however, was not asking a simple, "How ya doin'?" question, as Elijah supposed. The Lord was asking Elijah, "What is your life's purpose? What is your mission? Why are you here instead of out there accomplishing my plans for your life?"

Knowing that Elijah was completely missing the point, God sent him through a simple exercise to teach Elijah how to hear the voice in the midst of crisis. The Lord knew that this was Elijah's only hope of being revived and restored. Elijah needed to refocus. He must learn to listen and be attentive, no matter what was going on around him. Then he would experience personal revival in the middle of his difficulty.

Here is what God did:

And he said, Go forth, and stand upon the mount before the LORD. And, behold, the LORD passed by, and a great and strong wind rent the mountains, and brake in pieces the rocks before the LORD; but the LORD was not in the wind: and after the wind an earthquake; but the LORD was not in the earthquake: And after the earthquake a fire; but the LORD was not in the fire: and after the fire a still small voice.

1 Kings 19:11-12

Elijah stood on the mountain and felt the powerful wind of God blow, he felt the earth begin to shake, and he saw the fire of heaven fall, but God was not in any of those grand events. Finally he heard the still small voice of God. That voice whispered to him, the same voice that on so many occasions whispered to him in the nighttime hours. That voice stirred something on the inside of him that drew him out of the cave where he had been hiding.

Elijah began to become reacquainted with himself and with who God had made him to be. He wrapped his face in his mantle and walked toward the voice of God. The mantle denotes his calling, his gifting. His mantle was a reminder of his destiny and his purpose on earth. Elijah, drawn by the whisper of the Lord, was no longer going to allow his future to be filtered through the eyes of the flesh. His true identity was what God said about him, not what his detractors or enemies said about him. His true purpose was in the hands of God, not in his own finite ability to comprehend every circumstance.

Elijah realized that he must filter every experience through the mantle of his destiny. Only then would he see a personal revival in his crisis. This time when God asked what Elijah was doing there (verse 13), the Spirit of the Lord was able to turn Elijah around and point him toward his mission, knowing that he would respond with a renewed confidence because he once again had heard the word of the Lord.

His personal revival did not come in some grand overwhelming fashion. It came as he heard the whisper of God restoring back to him his true identity. He had forgotten, for just a moment in time, who he was in God. This lapse sent him into a major crisis. But with the gentle prodding of God, he was able to regain his focus, get back on track, and face the future with a renewed faith and commitment.

After this dramatic experience Elijah finds Elisha—Elisha who will eventually receive the double portion, the same Elisha who will do twice as many miracles as Elijah.

Like Elijah you sometimes face internal crises after the completion of one phase of your life. Yet like Elijah, you are not finished! There are others who need what you have. Your crisis is just giving you the fuel to get there!

16 A FRIEND OF SINNERS

Don't curse your crisis:
it will open your eyes to the needs of others

The crowd moved quickly through the streets of Jerusalem as the early morning sun pierced the sky. Some were just going along to see the show, others had a clear-cut agenda. The crowd seemed to grow larger as they neared the temple where Jesus was teaching. As they burst through the door, they thrust the only unwilling participant of this procession into the forefront. There, standing before Jesus and this large crowd, was a disheveled woman. Near her stood the scribes and Pharisees.

This unnamed woman was caught in a power struggle that she had nothing to do with. That struggle, however, thrust her into the midst of a crisis that she little anticipated. The religious leaders wanted to test Jesus on His commitment to the law. In order to do that they needed a human guinea pig who could be trapped in an egregious sin. They set the trap; she took the bait; and now she stood before an angry mob that wanted to strip her of her already flagging dignity. Then they wanted to take her life.

At this point, the Pharisees made their case to Jesus:

> *Master, this woman was taken in adultery, in the very act. Now Moses in the law commanded us, that such should be stoned: but what sayest thou?*
>
> John 8:4–5

Now they had Jesus. How could He deny the clear-cut decree of the law of Moses? He had to agree with them! The zeal and passion of the scribes and Pharisees toward the letter of the law was apparent, but so too was their blindness to the loving character of God. They were willing to destroy an already hurting person in order to make their religious point.

How Jesus handles the hurting

Have you ever faced an angry crowd who was more intent on making their point than healing your wounds? Have you ever felt like this woman, surrounded by clenched teeth and open Bibles? It seems that only heaven can help us if we get on the wrong side of an issue with some Christians. We have all met people whose passion for God is merely an extension of their anger at life.

Jesus, however, was about to introduce this hurting woman to the mercy of God and He was going to teach the religious leaders a lesson at the same time.

They continued to pester Him as He wrote in the sand, pretending to be distracted. He then stood up and said to them, *"He that is without sin among you, let him first cast a stone at her"* (John 8:7).

I can imagine a hush fell upon the religious leaders as each of them experienced conviction. Then, from the oldest to the youngest, they all walked away, leaving Jesus standing alone with the woman.

Jesus wasn't angry with her concerning her sin, as some portray Him to be, but He did not ignore the problem either. She had been dragged out of bed, paraded through the streets, and set up as an object of humiliation. What could Jesus say that would soothe her pain while at the same time address this important issue?

After everyone had gone, Jesus said to her, *"Woman, where are those thine accusers? hath no man condemned thee?"* When she said that no one was there to condemn her, Jesus simply told her, *"Neither do I condemn thee: go, and sin no more"* (John 8:10-11).

When we go through crisis, even if it is a crisis that we had a hand in creating, we experience the mercy of God. He follows that with truth, which then sets us free. That was how Jesus operated, speaking a redemptive, restorative word into people's greatest needs. He never excused sin, but He never left them feeling less than when He met them.

> **When we go through a crisis, even if it is a crisis that we had a hand in creating, we experience the mercy of God.**

In fact, just the opposite usually occurred. He usually made a deposit of hope into people's otherwise hopeless situations. When He went to the well of Samaria, He found a woman caught in a cycle of destructive relationships. She had been married and divorced five times and she was now living with a man who was not her husband. How she must have been struggling with years of rejection, self-loathing, and fear of any future commitment.

This was the essence of the Samaritan woman (John 4:7-42), yet not once in their conversation do we find a hint of judgment or condemnation. His love was not lost on this hurting woman. She knew that most men, especially Jewish men, would regard her as unclean. She would be considered a social outcast and they would have nothing to do with her; but Jesus talked with her about the deepest secrets of her heart. He truly cared about her, and that was more than she could imagine.

He looked past the circumstances and saw her potential, and that made an immediate impact. Her life was instantly transformed as she accepted His invitation to partake of the eternal, living water that He was offering. In fact, she was so touched by this simple event that she quickly went into the city and spread the news that the Messiah was at the well.

Evidence of His love

I believe that there are two essential lessons that we can learn from this simple story of the Samaritan woman at the well with Jesus:

#1—**God is redemptive in nature.** He knows our history; He understands the nature of our crisis; and He cares anyway. We are not alone in our battle. His arms are open wide and He is declaring to us: *"Come unto me, all ye that labour and are heavy laden, and I will give you rest"* (Matthew 11:28).

Can you hear His voice calling? Can you sense His Spirit rising up within you even in the midst of your struggle? He wants you to exchange your burden for His strength; your darkness for His light; your despair for His joy.

He wants us to know that our difficulties do not have to be the death of our dreams, our hope, or our future. *He is here to strengthen us and give us a new date with destiny regardless of the circumstances that are surrounding us.*

After all, John 16:33 does say, *"These things I have spoken unto you, that in me ye might have peace. In the world ye shall have tribulation: but be of good cheer; I have overcome the world."*

#2—God touches us so we can become a catalyst for others to be transformed as well. Can we believe that? Is it possible that the Lord will cause our crisis to work together for our good and for the good of others?

I believe that we must begin to see our crisis as a brand new opportunity for ministry. After all, who better to touch the lives of hurting people than someone who can relate to the pain of another? We are now uniquely qualified to become a healer to others because we have endured the pain of the cross ourselves.

Is not this what Jesus told Peter to do after he was restored from his own peculiar trial? Jesus said, *"Simon, Simon, behold, Satan hath desired to have you, that he may sift you as wheat: But I have prayed for thee, that thy faith fail not: and when thou art converted, strengthen thy brethren"* (Luke 22:31-32).

Benefits of pain and suffering

The Apostle Paul was no stranger to trials and affliction. The list of things that he endured would take several pages to explain. He was shipwrecked, beaten, left for dead, and imprisoned, just to name a few. However, he came out of each of those experiences with a very positive perspective on crisis. As he wrote to the church of Corinth, he revealed his insights into the purpose of pain and suffering:

> *Blessed be God, even the Father of our Lord Jesus Christ, the Father of mercies, and the God of all comfort; Who comforteth us in all our tribulation, that we may be able to comfort them which are in any trouble, by the comfort wherewith we ourselves are comforted of God.*

2 Corinthians 1:3-4

The scriptural evidence is clear. Pain, suffering, crisis, tribulation, whatever label that we wish to put upon it, *has a positive purpose in our lives!* So often we lose hope during our difficulty because we feel that we are now disqualified from ever being useful to God or anyone else ever again. *The exact opposite is true!* By allowing God to comfort us in our crisis, we are now more qualified than ever before to reach out and touch those who are hurting. What is it about those who have been wounded that enables them to better minister to others who are in a trial? The answer is twofold.

#1—Affliction has a way of showing us our own frailties and our own imperfections. We can no longer stand on Mt. Olympus handing down dogmatic decrees that have little or no experiential value. Too often, before our own crisis, we could very easily slip into a pharisaic attitude of superiority and judgment.

This attitude sends a signal to those who are hurting that their faith is somehow "weak" because they are suffering. We are like the disciples who said to Jesus about a man who was born blind: *"Master, who did sin, this man, or his parents, that he was born blind?"* (John 9:2).

This is not compassion at all, and those who are in the middle of a crisis can sense the duplicity in our demeanor as we are trying to figure out where they have failed. We often come off as someone who is attempting to bow down to these poor wayward people whose faith is not equal to the difficulties of life. Is it any wonder that there is very little healing occurring at this level?

The ones who have been tested through their own crisis have been freed from the pretense of self-perfection. They have felt the sting of rejection, failure,

> **Is it possible that the Lord will cause our crisis to work together for our good and for the good of others?**

and loneliness. They now know that it is not an issue of superiority versus inferiority. It has to do with the real, life-changing, gut-wrenching effects of pain. Those who are in the midst of pain need comfort just as the healer needed comfort when he or she was in pain.

Crisis-tested individuals stop asking the "whys" of the crisis and move on to the more important question of: "What can I do to lift the awesome burden that is crushing this struggling individual?" They can now comfort others because they themselves have been comforted.

#2—Before crisis we expend so much energy trying to impress others, meet their expectations, and achieve our own unattainable standards. This process becomes exhausting because we know within ourselves how far short we are falling. As a result, we begin to wear a mask in front of others for fear that if they really knew who we were they would reject us.

Crisis changes all that. It has a way of stripping off the mask and helping us focus on the important issues of life. When we go through a life-threatening trial, we drop the non-important issues. We no longer expend great amounts of energy on trivial things.

What great freedom this can bring when all is said and done! We slowly begin to rest in God's grace and we begin to care less and less how others feel about us or what others expect from us. As a result, we can identify with and make every effort to help others who are afraid and imperfect.

Remember how the Pharisees looked down their religious nose at Jesus because He was constantly hanging around with sinners? They felt that if He were truly spiritual that He needed to be above the fray; He needed to distance Himself from the sin and pain of the people (Matthew 9:10-12).

Jesus just didn't seem to have the need to impress others. He understood the primary focus of God: hurting people are God's purpose, not religious show, public spectacle, or the applause of man.

How did Jesus learn this lesson? How did He become obedient to the real plan of God? The same way we do: *"Though he were a Son, yet learned he obedience by the things which he suffered"* (Hebrews 5:8).

Let each of us pray, "God, help me to see your grand design in the midst of my crisis. Allow me to have a new perspective in all that I am going through. Comfort me by your Holy Spirit in all my afflictions and then strengthen me for the task of comforting others in their afflictions. Give me grace and peace and hope that I may then extend it to those who need it most."

Amen!

17 TAKING DOMINION IN THE STORM

Don't curse your crisis:
it will provide opportunity to take dominion

The ability to continue to believe God when surrounded by adverse circumstances is a function of what we call faith. Knowing God's purposes remain, we hold to them even when their fulfillment is delayed and the avenues to achieving them escape us. Throughout our walk with Him, God lays firmly in our spirits an unshakable and an unsinkable foundation. At different seasons in our lives shaking and storms may arise so that which cannot be shaken might remain. When you realize that God has purposed you for dominion you refuse to accept the role of spectator. You quit being a passenger in life and you start driving.

Paul, the Apostle, had made frequent references to his belief that he would go to Rome and preach. Though it did not happen immediately, it was sure to be. He occupied himself in the meantime by continuing to preach to the people everywhere he went. By the time we read Acts chapter 25 we find him being falsely accused. And feeling it necessary to appeal his case to Caesar, he was put on a ship—destination Italy.

Isn't it amazing how the enemy can act as if he owns you—to dare to act as if he, not God, is in charge of you? Even when the accuser thinks he is working against you, God turns it to further you into His divine plan!

Yet still it seems that the man of God should arrive in Italy in a better fashion than being a prisoner in the lower decks of the boat. As God's servants we have the promise of freedom, and not to be beneath but above only. When limitations are trying to be placed upon you and you are displaced in life, crisis may come to free you from limitation and provide you with the opportunity to take dominion.

Paul warned the sailors of impending doom. His advice was ignored. The storm came; the crisis took control. Yet in the midst of crisis Paul received a word. He was destined to preach in Rome! The storm couldn't stop it. And since he was on board their ship, he was not a spectator, but he had dominion.

Listen to these words:

For there stood by me this night the angel of God, whose I am, and whom I serve, Saying, Fear not, Paul; thou must be brought before Caesar: and, lo, God hath given thee all them that sail with thee. Wherefore, sirs, be of good cheer: for I believe God, that it shall be even as it was told me.

Acts 27:23-25

Can you see it? God had actually given Paul those who sailed with him. He begins the journey as one who is sailing with them. Since they have the issue of authority backward the crisis comes to correct this. Storms and shaking are no cause for fear when your foundation is unshakable and your faith is unsinkable.

In the darkest hour

If we feel chained to a bad job, a bad situation, a bad marriage, etc., God has a plan to bring His dominion in our lives into focus. Whatever the problem, be of good cheer (as Paul said) because the storm will not get you. God will not let you drown in the sea.

Even if things look the darkest, like they couldn't get any worse, hang on! That is when things are about to break through. You may not know how you got there or how it will all work out, but you do know that God will bring you through. Hang on to the blood of the Lamb and the word of your testimony. Hang on, God will bring you out.

Around midnight on the fourteenth day lost at sea, the sailors (who were given to Paul) sensed that the water was getting shallower. They were nearing land! It is interesting to note that the fourteenth day is also the day of Passover. The children of Israel put blood over the doorposts of their houses at midnight when things were the darkest, but liberty was just around the corner!

As the 276 men on board were waiting for the sun to rise, Paul told them to eat. They needed nourishment and he broke bread with them. All still looked lost, but Paul praised God for His goodness in the midst of it. As a result, everyone made it safely to shore; only the boat was lost.

In the middle of the storm

God is bringing dominion through the storm, so praise Him during the storm. Those around you will know that God is able and mighty to heal, deliver, and save you.

I believe the ship represents the world's message. The centurion who was ordered to guard Paul is representative of people who are obedient to the master of the world's system. And Paul represents the Christians who enter the world's system but are not of it and whose actions state, "I'm just on board to take over. I have dominion. You think I'm below, but God has a way of using things to show His way as true."

> The shaking around you is not there to harm you, but to bring you to the position of dominion and authority.

Just as Paul's boat could not handle the storm, so the boats (plans, ideas, beliefs, etc.) that people create today will not make it through the storm. *The only way to get through is to believe the Word that God has spoken to you.*

Don't trust in the boat. Sooner or later we had better put our trust in God because that is the only way through the storm.

In the middle of the storm, break bread and give thanks. God is good and He's on your side working in your favor. The joy of the Lord is your strength. Most likely you will have to battle fear. It will try to paralyze you and stop you from praising God. If your praise stops, you'll lose your joy, and if you lose your joy, you'll lose your strength. If you lose your strength, you can't fight, and if you can't fight, you can't win.

Stand up and say, "God, I will thank you regardless." Praise Him for your breath, for peace, for life, etc. You may not know how the storm will stop, but who cares! Find a cause to praise Him in the middle of it.

You may not understand it, but God rules and reigns regardless. You can trust Him that you will never be ashamed, moved, or lost. The boat might be lost, but the people will be saved. God is always working on your behalf, even in the midst of your crisis.

So don't curse your crisis!

IN CONCLUSION

No volume of words or cleverly printed phrases can release the pain and pressure crisis brings. Ultimately, the experiences and advice of others fall short when we find ourselves dealing with the reality of shattering events. The words in this book, however, were written to let you know you are not alone in your crisis! Everyone is going to experience it. And hopefully these words serve as a kind of survival road map to help you keep your wits about you when you feel as though you are coming apart at the seams.

This has not been meant as some trivial "Look for the good" ideology, but rather a "Look for God" theology. That is to say in all of life's difficulties, God somehow enters into them, turning them, using them, and yes, even building you with them. These words were written not to attach you to crisis, but to liberate you from the negative emotions and effects troubled times bring. Liberation is the goal. Freedom comes when I realize I cannot manipulate life; therefore I do not have to wait for perfect circumstances to serve God, be glad, or succeed. I have in the midst of uncertain days a certain faith, an unwavering joy, and a consistent committed God.

It is this knowledge that gives us hope. It is this assurance that makes us strong. It is His faithfulness that keeps us, His love that upholds us. Fear must go. Trouble must go. His purpose is sure; His promises yes and Amen!

God is our refuge and strength, a very present help in trouble. Therefore will not we fear, though the earth be

removed, and though the mountains be carried into the
midst of the sea;

Psalm 46:1-2

Don't curse your crisis; things have a way of working out!